Lecture Notes in Computer Science 8912

Commenced Publication in 1973
Founding and Former Series Editors:
Gerhard Goos, Juris Hartmanis, and Jan van Leeuwen

More information about this series at http://www.springer.com/series/7412

Qiang Ji · Thomas B. Moeslund
Gang Hua · Kamal Nasrollahi (Eds.)

Face and Facial Expression Recognition from Real World Videos

International Workshop, Stockholm
Sweden, August 24, 2014
Revised Selected Papers

 Springer

Editors
Qiang Ji
Computer and Systems Engineering
Pensselaer Polytechnic Institute
Troy, New York
USA

Gang Hua
Department of Computer Science
Stevens Institute of Technology
Hoboken, New Jersey
USA

Thomas B. Moeslund
Department of Architecture, Design, and
    Media Technology
Aalborg
Denmark

Kamal Nasrollahi
Department of Architecture, Design, and
    Media Technology
Aalborg
Denmark

ISSN 0302-9743   ISSN 1611-3349   (electronic)
Lecture Notes in Computer Science
ISBN 978-3-319-13736-0   ISBN 978-3-319-13737-7   (eBook)
DOI 10.1007/978-3-319-13737-7

Library of Congress Control Number: 2015935627

LNCS Sublibrary: SL6 – Image Processing, Computer Vision, Patttern Recognition, and Graphics

Springer Cham Heidelberg New York Dordrecht London

Printed on acid-free paper

Springer International Publishing AG Switzerland is part of Springer Science+Business Media
(www.springer.com)

Preface

The face plays an important role in many computer vision applications, like surveillance systems, human-computer interaction, gaming, remote monitoring of patients at home, etc. This is because the detected faces in such applications, can not only be used for human identification, but also for many other purposes, like expression recognition. The current technologies employed in facial analysis systems in these mentioned areas are rapidly progressing. This has been the main motivation for organizing a workshop to bring together researchers working on different topics related to face and facial expression recognition. FFER, International Workshop on Face and Facial Expression Recognition from Real World Videos, has been organized to serve exactly this point.

FFER 2014 was held in conjunction with the 22nd International Conference on Pattern Recognition in Stockholm, Sweden, on August 24, 2014. For this first occurrence of FFER we received 11 valid submissions. The received papers went through a rigorous blind-reviewing process, at least two reviewers per paper, by a Program Committee consisting of leading world experts in the field. This resulted in nine accepted papers. These accepted papers have been organized in to the following subtopics: face recognition, face alignment and facial expression recognition, and other applications of facial images. For each of these subtopics, we also collected an invited paper which identifies the beginning of a new section in these proceedings.

The high quality of the papers in these proceedings are results of first the authors who had submitted their works to FFER, and then the reviewers who had carefully checked the quality of the papers and had provided valuable feedback to the authors for improving their papers before publication.

We were very pleased to have Prof. Massimo Tistarelli from University of Sassari in Italy to give the invited talk for the workshop on Face Recognition: Challenges, Applications, and Some New Technologies.

We would like to express our sincere thanks to the local organizers of ICPR 2014, who helped us to make FFER a successful workshop. Finally, we are thankful to Springer's LNCS staff and editors for supporting the publication of these proceedings.

Looking forward to meeting you in the next FFER.

October 2014

Qiang Ji
Thomas B. Moeslund
Gang Hua
Kamal Nasrollahi

Organization

Organizers

Qiang Ji	Rensselaer Polytechnic Institute, USA
Thomas B. Moeslund	Aalborg University, Denmark
Gang Hua	Stevens Institute of Technology, USA
Kamal Nasrollahi	Aalborg University, Denmark

Invited Speaker

Massimo Tistarelli	University of Sassari, Italy

Program Committee (Reviewers)

Abdenour Hadid	University of Oulu, Finland
Abhinav Dhall	Australian National University, Australia
Albert Salah	Boğaziçi University, Turkey
Andrea Lagorio	University of Sassari, Italy
Anil Jain	Michigan State University, USA
Guosheng Yang	Minzu University of China, China
Jose Alba-Castro	University of Vigo, Spain
Josef Kittler	University of Surrey, UK
Karl Ricanek	University of North Carolina Wilmington, USA
Lijun Yin	Binghamton University, USA
Marios Savvides	Carnegie Mellon University, USA
Rama Chellappa	University of Maryland, USA
Shangfei Wang	University of Science and Technology of China, China
Shaogang Gong	Queen Mary University of London, UK
Sudeep Sarkar	University of South Florida, USA
Vladimir Pavlovic	Rutgers University, USA
Xiaofei He	Zhejiang University, China
Xiaoming Liu	Michigan State University, USA
Xilin Chen	Chinese of Academy of Sciences, China
Yan Tong	University of South Carolina, USA
Yan Shuicheng	National University of Singapore, Singapore
Yun Fu	Northeastern University, USA

Supported by

International Association of Pattern Recognition (IAPR)

COST Action IC1106

Contents

Face Recognition

Probabilistic Elastic Part Model for Real-World Face Recognition

Gang Hua[✉]

Department of Computer Science, Stevens Institute of Technology,
Castle Point on Hudson, Hoboken, NJ 07030, USA
ghua@stevens.edu

Abstract. The ever popularity of online social media, and the ubiquity of video cameras, provide an unique source of information that is otherwise not available for military, security, and forensics applications. As a result, robust recognition of the faces presented in these unconstrained images and videos became an emerging need. For example, both the Vancouver (Canada) Riots 2011, and the tragedy Boston Bombing 2013, called for robust facial recognition technologies to identify the suspects from low quality images and videos from unconstrained sources.

In this paper, we briefly summarize our work on probabilistic elastic part model, which produces a pose invariant and compact representation for both image and video faces. The model produces a fixed dimension representation no matter how many frames a video face contains. This allows the representations produced from video faces of arbitrary frame numbers to be directly compared without the need of computationally expensive frame-to-frame matching. The probabilistic elastic part model produces state-of-the-art results in several real-world face recognition benchmarks, which we will also briefly discuss.

1 Introduction

The ever popularity of online social media, and the ubiquity of video cameras, provide an unique source of information that is otherwise not available for military, security, and forensics applications. As a result, robust recognition of the faces presented in these unconstrained images and videos became an emerging need. For example, both the Vancouver (Canada) Riots 2011, and the tragedy Boston Bombing 2013, called for robust facial recognition technologies to identify the suspects from low quality images and videos from unconstrained sources.

Face recognition in these unconstrained visual sources is far from solved. Under well-constrained setting, *i.e.*, when the face photos are taken from frontal view in mobile studio or mugshot environment, state-of-the-art face recognition system in the Multiple Biometrics Evaluation (MBE) 2010 [1] reported a verification rate of 0.997 at the false alarm rate of 1 out of 1000. While in the most recent Point and Shoot Video Face and Person Recognition Competition [2], state-of-the-art verification rate is 0.26 at the false acceptance rate of 1 out of 100 (achieved by the algorithm from the PI's group [3]).

© Springer International Publishing Switzerland 2015
Q. Ji et al. (Eds.): FFER 2014, LNCS 8912, pp. 3–10, 2015.
DOI: 10.1007/978-3-319-13737-7_1

We argue that the core to further push the frontier of large scale face recognition in the wild is to develop a comprehensive, compact, and yet flexible representation of a face subject. By comprehensive, we mean that it shall integrate the visual information from all relevant visual sources (even those from different visual spectrum) of a subject to better model the visual variations. By compact, we mean that it is scalable both in terms of computing and storage. By flexible, we mean that it can be incrementally updated, either incorporating new observations, or retiring obsolete observations, without the need to revisit all the video frames used to build the original representation.

In this short technical report, we discuss our recent work on probabilistic elastic part model for real-world face recognition, which has produced state-of-the-art results in several face recognition benchmarks [3–6].

2   The Probabilistic Elastic Part Model

The PEP model produces a pose invariant representation for real-world face recognition. Pose variation is a major challenge that hinders face understanding. Both the early work on Eigenfaces [7] and illumination cones [8] have shown that when faces are appropriately aligned, they can be modeled by a linear subspace. But when pose varies, this is no longer true.[1] Since illumination (except extreme ones) can largely be addressed by local invariant descriptors, we focus on representations that are robust to pose changes. We use *unsupervised learning* to learn the representations rather than define the representation around landmark points [9].

Our PEP model presents an unified representation for both image and video based face recognition. Its current recognition accuracy is ranked **NO.1** in the YouTube Faces Database (YTFD) [10], **NO.1** under the most restricted protocol in the Labeled Faces in the Wild (LFW) dataset [11], where no external training data is exploited. It is also the **top performing algorithm** in the recent PaSC Video Face and Person Recognition Competition [2,3]. In [5], we proposed an unsupervised detector adaptation algorithm with the PEP representation. It achieved the **top** detection accuracy on the challenging Face Detection Dataset and Benchmark (FDDB) [12].

The PEP model [3–6] learns a spatial-appearance (*i.e.*, a local descriptor augmented by its location) Gaussian mixture model. By constraining the Gaussian components to be spherical, the PEP model balances the impact of the spatial and appearance parts and forces the allocation of a Gaussian component to each local region of the image. Given densely extracted spatial-appearance local descriptors at multiple scales from training face images, we learn parameters using Expectation-Maximization (EM). The third column of Figure 1 shows some of the Gaussian PEP components (group of image patches assigned to the same Gaussian component) learned from the LFW dataset [13].

---

[1] It is notable that none of the numerous subspace and manifold modeling methods that directly model image pixels have achieved competitive performance on real-world face databases.

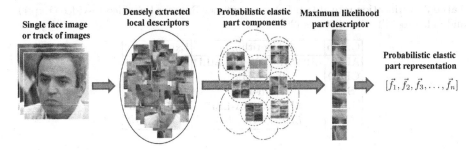

Fig. 1. The pipeline for producing the PEP representation

Table 1. Performance on the most restricted LFW

Algorithm	Accuracy ± Error(%)
V1/MKL[14]	79.35 ± 0.55
Fisher vector[15]	87.47 ± 1.49
PEP	90.40 ± 1.33
A-PEP	**91.00 ± 1.44**

Table 2. Performance on YouTube Faces Dataset

Algorithm	Accuracy ± Error(%)
DDML [16]	82.3 ± 1.5
VF^2 [17]	84.7 ± 1.4
PEP	87.72 ± 1.22
A-PEP	**88.04 ± 1.22**

Figure 1 illustrates the pipeline for producing the PEP representation for either a face image or a set/track of face images. Each Gaussian component of the model selects the image descriptor with highest likelihood for that component. For example, if a particular Gaussian component tends to model nose-like patterns, then the chosen patch will tend to be on the subject's nose. The final representation is a simple concatentation of the selected descriptors from all components. Since the positions of patches are part of the descriptors, the chosen descriptor must necessarily come from a region near the component's mean. With k face parts of dimension d (*i.e.*, k Gaussian components), the descriptor describing the whole face has $k \times d$ elements.

The PEP representation presents three advantages over existing representations for face recognition:

- It generates a single fixed-dimension representation given a varying number of face images from a person. This is important as it avoids expensive frame-to-frame matching.
- When building the representation from multiple face images, it integrates the visual information from all these face images together instead of selecting a single best frame.
- It is additive, *i.e.*, when additional face images of one specific person are available, the representation can be updated without the images that produced the original representation.

The PEP representation has been applied to both face verification [2–4,6] and unsupervised face detector adaptation [5] in the PI's recent work. We summarize the results below.

Table 3. Verification rate at 0.01 False Acceptance Rate for the video-to-video (Exp.1) and video-to-still (Exp.2) tasks [2]

Group	Algorithm	Exp.1	Exp.2
ADSC	LBP-SIFT-WPCA-SILD	0.09	0.23
CPqD	ISV-GMM	0.05	0.11
SIT	**Eigen-PEP**	**0.26**	**0.24**
Ljub	PLDA-WPCA-LLR	0.19	0.26
CSU	*LRPCA Baseline*	*0.08*	*0.10*

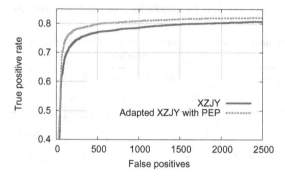

Fig. 2. Performance comparison on *FDDB* by adapting the XZJY face detector

Face Verification. For face verification, the PEP model can be used in two different ways. The first is to directly generate the PEP representation; the second is to adapt the PEP model to *each pair of faces* to be verified through a Bayesian EM algorithm, where we adapt the PEP model to better fit the input faces while ensuring that the adapted model, A-PEP, does not deviate too much from the universally trained PEP model.

We first report results on both the LFW and the YouTube Faces Database, as shown in Table 1 and Table 2. At this time, the verification accuracy of the A-PEP model is ranked **first** on both the YouTube Faces Database and the "most restricted protocol" for the LFW data set, where no external data is used.

Based on the PEP model, we further developed the Eigen-PEP representation [3], which is the **winning algorithm** on the video-to-video matching task in the recent PaSC Video Face and Person Recognition Competition [2]. We summarize the results in Table 3. The PEP model ranked **NO.1** in the video-to-video task, leading the second best by a significant margin, *i.e.*, 0.26 *v.s.* 0.19 verification rate under 0.01 false acceptance rate. It also ranked **NO.2** in the video-to-still task, which is only slightly lower than the best performing one, *i.e.* 0.24 *v.s.* 0.26 under 0.01 false acceptance rate.

Unsupervised Face Detector Adaptation. PI Hua's ICCV 2013 unsupervised detector adaptation algorithm based on the PEP representation [5] demonstrates that *the PEP representation is also discriminative in differentiating faces*

from non-face images. The general adaptation method can be applied to any off-the-shelf face detector, and sets a new FDDB [12] accuracy record by adapting the state-of-the-art XZJY exemplar-based face detector [18]. (See Figure 2.)

3   Related Work

We discuss related works adopted GMM for visual recognition [19–22] and briefly review the current state-of-the-art face verification algorithms on both the LFW [14,23–32] and YouTube Faces dataset [10].

The Gaussian mixture model has been widely used for various visual recognition tasks including face recognition [19,21,22] and scene recognition [19,20]. While early works [21,22] focused on modeling the holistic appearance of the face with GMM, more recent works [19,20] have largely exploited the bag of local descriptors representation and use GMM to model the local appearances of the image.

In their frameworks, a GMM is the probabilistic representation of an image. Then the GMM is encoded into a super-vector representation for classification. In our work, the universally trained GMM is a probabilistic general representation of human face, where each Gaussian component models the spatial-appearance distribution of a facial part.

In terms of model adaptation, Zhou *et al.* [19] also leveraged the GMM and Bayesian adaptation paradigm to learn adaptive representations, wherein the super-vector representations are adopted for building the final classification model. However, none of these works conducted joint spatial-appearance modeling using spherical Gaussians as the mixture components and their Bayesian adaptation is applied to a single image whereas we conduct a joint Bayesian adaptation on a pair of faces/face tracks to better build the correspondences of the local descriptors in the two face images/face tracks.

One of the specialty of the PEP-model is the spherical Gaussian components. We rarely see previous literatures explicitly address the unbalanced dimensionality between appearance and spatial constraint for spatial-augmented descriptor. A GMM with regular Gaussian components trained over the spatial-appearance features may not be desirable for building the PEP-model because face structures can be similar in appearance but vary spatially, *e.g.*, left eye and right eye, could be mixed into the same Gaussian component under weak spatial constraint, as the dimensionality of the spatial location is relatively smaller comparing to the size of the appearance descriptor. While we use a GMM with spherical Gaussian components in the PEP-model, the strength of spatial constraint can be tuned by scaling the location units which help balance the influence of appearance and spatial constraint in learning the facial parts.

In addition to the related works adopted GMM, here we also briefly discuss some top performers over two widely evaluated face verification datasets. A number of previous works on image-based face verification reported their performance on the Labeled Faces in the Wild dataset (LFW). The LFW benchmark has well-defined protocols. We focus on the *image-restricted with no outside data* protocol which does not allow any additional datasets to be used for face alignment, feature extraction, or building the recognition model. The current state-of-the-art under the same protocol is the fisher vector faces presented by Simonyan *et al.* [15], which achieved an average accuracy of 0.8747 ± 0.0149. Our method significantly improves the average accuracy to be 0.9100 ± 0.0144.

Predominant recent works focused on the other protocols [24, 27–32], which have pushed the recognition accuracy to be as high as 0.9852. They all leveraged additional data sources or powerful face alignment algorithms trained from external data sources. We focus our experiments on the most restricted protocol on LFW as our interest is the design of a robust face representation for pose variant face verification. Besides the fact that our method does not exploit any outside training data or side information, the PEP model and representation, not only is flexible to local descriptor choices that it could benefit from special local descriptors; but also could address residual misalignments so that it can complement and benefit from a good face alignment system.

Restricting the evaluation to the most restricted protocol enables objective evaluation of the capacity of the PEP model and representation. The PEP representation only employed simple visual features such as LBP and SIFT. We also observed consistent improvement when fusing the results from these two types of features together, suggesting that we can further improve face recognition accuracy from the PEP model and representation by fusing more types of features, or by feature learning, which will be part of the work in this project.

While a number of state-of-the-art methods on LFW may not be applicable to the video-based face verification directly without resorting to the computationally expensive frame-to-frame matching, our work can handle the video-based setting without modification. Wolf *et al.* [10] published a video face verification benchmark, namely YouTube Faces, is widely recognized and evaluated these years.

There can be various ways to interpret the video-based setting. Wolf *et al.* [10, 33] treat each video as a set of face images and compute set-to-set similarity; Zhen *et al.* [34] takes a spatial-temporal block based representation for each video and utilizes multiple face region descriptors within a metric learning framework. In the PEP model and representation, we have a consistent visual representation for both videos and images. Without exploiting temporal information or extra reference/background dataset, we build correspondences between face parts across frames with the PEP-model. Our algorithm outperforms all the state-of-the-art methods on the YouTube faces dataset under the same protocol by a large margin.

4   Conclusion

In summary, PEP is a top performer for both image and video based face verification, and face detection, in real-world images and videos from unconstrained sources. It advances the state-of-the-art facial recognition technology for large scale image based biometrics identification in unconstrained image and video sources. We anticipate future research built on top of the PEP model would drive for a more comprehensive understanding of the faces towards human level robustness and accuracy for real-world face recognition.

References

1. Grother, P.J., Quinn, G.W., Phillips, P.J.: Mbe 2010: report on the evaluation of 2d still-image face recognition algorithms. Technical Report NISTIR 7709, National Institute of Standards and Technology (2010)
2. Beveridge, R., Flynn, P., Philips, J., Zhang, H., Liong, V.E., Lu, J., Angeloni, M., Pereira, T., Li, H., Hua, G., Struc, V., Krizaj, J.: The ijcb 2014 pasc video face and person recognition competition. In: Submitted to International Joint Conf. on Biometrics, Clearwater, FL (2014)
3. Li, H., Hua, G., Lin, Z., Shen, X., Brandt, J.: Eigen-pep for video face recognition. In: Proc. The Twelvth Asian Conference on Computer Vision, Singapore (2014)
4. Li, H., Hua, G., Lin, Z., Brandt, J., Yang, J.: Probabilistic elastic matching for pose variant face verification. In: Proc. IEEE Conf. on Computer Vision and Pattern Recognition, Portland, Oregon (2013)
5. Li, H., Hua, G., Lin, Z., Brandt, J., Yang, J.: Probabilistic elastic part model for unsupervised face detector adaptation. In: Proc. IEEE International Conference on Computer Vision, Sydney, Australia (2013)
6. Li, H., Hua, G.: Probabilistic elastic part model: a pose-invariant representation for real-world face verification. Submitted to IEEE Trans. on Pattern Analysis and Machine Intelligence (2014) (Under Review)
7. Turk, M.A., Pentland, A.P.: Face recognition using eigenfaces. In: Proc. of IEEE Conf. on Computer Vision and Patter Recognition, pp. 586–591 (1991)
8. Belhumeur, P., Kriegman, D.: What is the set of images of an object under all possible lighting conditions. In: CVPR, pp. 270–277 (1996)
9. Chen, D., Cao, X., Wen, F., Sun, J.: Blessing of dimisionality: high dimensional feature and its efficient compression for face verification. In: Proc. IEEE Conference on Computer Vision and Pattern Recognition (2013)
10. Wolf, L., Hassner, T., Maoz, I.: Face recognition in unconstrained videos with matched background similarity. In: Proc. IEEE Conference on Computer Vision and Pattern Recognition, pp. 529–534 (2011)
11. Huang, G.B., Ramesh, M., Berg, T., Learned-Miller, E.: Labeled faces in the wild: a database for studying face recognition in unconstrained environments. Technical Report 07–49, University of Massachusetts, Amherst (2007)
12. Jain, V., Learned-Miller, E.: FDDB: a benchmark for face detection in unconstrained settings. Technical Report UM-CS-2010-009, University of Massachusetts, Amherst (2010)
13. Huang, G.B., Jones, M.J., Learned-Miller, E.: Lfw results using a combined nowak plus merl recognizer. In: Faces in Real-Life Images Workshop in European Conference on Computer Vision (ECCV) (2008)
14. Pinto, N., DiCarlo, J.J., Cox, D.D.: How far can you get with a modern face recognition test set using only simple features? In: IEEE Computer Vision and Pattern Recognition (2009)
15. Simonyan, K., Parkhi, O.M., Vedaldi, A., Zisserman, A.: Fisher vector faces in the wild. In: British Machine Vision Conference (2013)
16. Hu, J., Lu, J., Tan, Y.P.: Discriminative deep metric learning for face verification in the wild. In: Proc. IEEE Conference on Computer Vision and Pattern Recognition (2014)
17. Parkhi, O.M., Simonyan, K., Vedaldi, A., Zisserman, A.: A compact and discriminative face track descriptor. In: Proc. IEEE Conference on Computer Vision and Pattern Recognition (2014)

18. Shen, X., Lin, Z., Brandt, J., Wu, Y.: Detecting and aligning faces by image retrieval. In: Proc. IEEE Conference on Computer Vision and Pattern Recognition (2013)

19. Zhou, X., Cui, N., Li, Z., Liang, F., Huang, T.: Hierarchical gaussianization for image classification. In: 2009 IEEE 12th International Conference on Computer Vision, pp. 1971–1977 (2009)

20. Dixit, M., Rasiwasia, N., Vasconcelos, N.: Adapted gaussian models for image classification. In: 2011 IEEE Conference on Computer Vision and Pattern Recognition (CVPR), pp. 937–943 (2011)

21. Gross, R., Yang, J., Waibel, A.: Growing gaussian mixture models for pose invariant face recognition. In: International Conference on Pattern Recognition, vol. 1, p. 5088 (2000)

22. Wang, X., Tang, X.: Bayesian face recognition based on gaussian mixture models. In: 17th International Conference on Proceedings of the Pattern Recognition, ICPR 2004, vol. 4, pp. 142–145. IEEE Computer Society, Washington, DC (2004)

23. Nowak, E., Jurie, F.: Learning visual similarity measures for comparing never seen objects. In: Proc. of IEEE Conf. on Computer Vision and Pattern Recognition, Minneapolis, MN (2007)

24. Kumar, N., Berg, A., Belhumeur, P.N., Nayar, S.: Describable visual attributes for face verification and image search. IEEE Trans. Pattern Anal. Mach. Intell. **33**, 1962–1977 (2011)

25. Wolf, L., Hassner, T., Taigman, Y.: Effective unconstrained face recognition by combining multiple descriptors and learned background statistics. IEEE Trans. Pattern Anal. Mach. Intell. **33**, 1978–1990 (2011)

26. Hua, G., Akbarzadeh, A.: A robust elastic and partial matching metric for face recognition. In: Proc. IEEE International Conference on Computer Vision, Kyoto, Japan (2009)

27. Cao, Z., Yin, Q., Tang, X., Sun, J.: Face recognition with learning-based descriptor. In: Proc. IEEE Conference on Computer Vision and Pattern Recognition, pp. 2707–2714 (2010)

28. Yin, Q., Tang, X., Sun, J.: An associate-predict model for face recognition. In: Proc. IEEE Conference on Computer Vision and Pattern Recognition, pp. 497–504 (2011)

29. Cox, D., Pinto, N.: Beyond simple features: a large-scale feature search approach to unconstrained face recognition. In: 2011 IEEE International Conference on Automatic Face Gesture Recognition and Workshops (FG 2011), pp. 8–15 (2011)

30. Wang, F., Guibas, L.J.: Supervised earth mover's distance learning and its computer vision applications. In: Proc. of European Conf. on Computer Vision, pp. 442–455 (2012)

31. Berg, T., Belhumeur, P.: Tom-vs-pete classifiers and identity-preserving alignment for face verification. In: Proceedings of the British Machine Vision Conference, pp. 129.1–129.11. BMVA Press (2012)

32. Lu, C., Tang, X.: Surpassing human-level face verification performance on lfw with gaussianface. CoRR (2014)

33. Wolf, L., Levy, N.: The svm-minus similarity score for video face recognition. In: Proc. IEEE Conf. on Computer Vision and Pattern Recognition, Porland, OR (2013)

34. Zhen, C., Li, W., Xu, D., Shan, S., Chen, X.: Fusing robust face region descriptors via multiple metric learning for face recognition in the wild. In: Proc. IEEE Conference on Computer Vision and Pattern Recognition (2013)

Local Feature Evaluation for a Constrained Local Model Framework

Maiya Hori(✉), Shogo Kawai, Hiroki Yoshimura, and Yoshio Iwai

Graduate School of Engineering, Tottori University,
101 Minami 4-chome, Koyama-cho, Tottori 680-8550, Japan
hori@ike.tottori-u.ac.jp

Abstract. We present local feature evaluation for a constrained local model (CLM) framework. We target facial images captured by a mobile camera such as a smartphone. When recognizing facial images captured by a mobile camera, changes in lighting conditions and image degradation from motion blur are considerable problems. CLM is effective for recognizing a facial expression because partial occlusions can be handled easily. In the CLM framework, the optimization strategy is local expert-based deformable model fitting. The likelihood of alignment at a particular landmark location is acquired beforehand using the local features of a large number of images and is used for estimating model parameters. In this learning phase, the features and classifiers used have a great influence on the accuracy of estimation in landmark locations. In our study, tracking accuracy can be improved by changing the features and classifiers for parts of the face. In the experiments, the likelihood map was generated using various features and classifiers, and the accuracy of landmark locations was compared with the conventional method.

1 Introduction

In recent years, communication robots [1] used in applications such as guidance and nursing care have been developed. These communication robots have a camera and a microphone and can communicate with the target by recognizing speech and facial expressions. Figure 1 shows a cellphone-type tele-operated communication medium called Elfoid [2]. Elfoid is designed to transmit the speaker's presence to the communication partner using a camera and microphone. When using this type of robot for communication, it is important to convey the facial expressions of the speaker to increase communication modality. If the speaker's facial movements can be regenerated accurately using these robots, the human presence can be adequately conveyed. Elfoid has a camera within its body and the speaker's facial movements can be estimated through an accurate facial recognition approach. When we recognize facial images captured by a mobile camera such as Elfoid, changes in lighting conditions and image degradation from motion blur are considerable problems. In this study, we aim to construct a face tracking technique that works robustly even under severe conditions.

© Springer International Publishing Switzerland 2015
Q. Ji et al. (Eds.): FFER 2014, LNCS 8912, pp. 11–19, 2015.
DOI: 10.1007/978-3-319-13737-7_2

Fig. 1. Cellphone-type tele-operated android: Elfoid. It is important to convey the facial expressions of the speaker to increase communication modality.

2   Related Work

Face tracking techniques using feature points such as the corners of the eyes and mouth are effective for recognition of facial expressions because a face is a non-rigid object. Deformable model fitting approaches [3][4] have been proposed. Facial deformable models can be divided into two main categories, holistic and part based models.

A notable example of a holistic model is the Active Appearance model (AAM) [3]. Holistic models employ a Point Distribution Model (PDM) as:

$$\mathbf{x_i} = s\mathbf{R}(\overline{\mathbf{x_i}} + \varPhi_i \mathbf{q}) + \mathbf{t}, \tag{1}$$

where $\mathbf{x_i}$ denotes the 2D location of the PDM's ith landmark, s denotes global scaling, $\mathbf{R}$ denotes a rotation and $\mathbf{t}$ denotes a translation. $\overline{\mathbf{x_i}}$ denotes the mean location of the ith PDM landmark in the reference frame and $\varPhi_i$ denotes the basis of the variations. $\mathbf{q}$ is a set of non-rigid parameters. A statistically shaped model is acquired from a set of training points by applying principal component analysis (PCA). The algorithm uses the difference between the current estimate of the shape model and the target image, to drive an optimization process. However, holistic approaches have many drawbacks. They are sensitive to lighting changes, and partial occlusions cannot be easily handled.

Part-based models use local image patches around the landmark points. Constrained Local Models[4] outperform AAM in terms of landmark localization accuracy. CLM fitting is generally posed as a search for the PDM parameters, $\mathbf{p}$, that minimize the misalignment error in following Eq. (2):

$$\mathcal{Q}(\mathbf{p}) = \mathcal{R}(\mathbf{p}) + \sum_{i=1}^{n} \mathcal{D}_i(\mathbf{x}_i; \mathcal{I}), \tag{2}$$

where $\mathcal{R}$ is a regularization term and $\mathcal{D}_i$ denotes the measure of misalignment for the ith landmark at $\mathbf{x}_i$ in the image $\mathcal{I}$. In the CLM framework the objective is to create a shape model from the parameters $\mathbf{p}$. In [4], the regularization and misalignment error function in Eq. (2) take the following forms:

$$\mathcal{R}(\mathbf{p}) = -\ln p(\mathbf{p}), \tag{3}$$

$$\mathcal{D}_i(\mathbf{x}_i; \mathcal{I}) = -\ln p(l_i = 1 | \mathbf{x_i}, \mathcal{I}). \tag{4}$$

CLM models the likelihood of alignment at a particular landmark location, $\mathbf{x}$, as follows:

$$\mathbf{p}(l_i = 1 | \mathbf{x}, \mathcal{I}) = \frac{1}{1 + \exp\{l_i \mathcal{C}_i(\mathbf{x}; \mathcal{I})\}}, \tag{5}$$

where $\mathcal{C}_i$ denotes a classifier that discriminates aligned from misaligned locations. The likelihood of alignment at a particular landmark location is acquired beforehand using local features of a large number of images. To generate the classifier $\mathcal{C}_i$, Saragih et al. [4] use logistic regression. Mean-shift vectors from each landmark are computed using the likelihood of alignment and the parameters $\mathbf{p}$ are updated. These processes are iterated until the parameters $\mathbf{p}$ converge.

When we recognize facial images captured by a mobile camera within Elfoid, changes in lighting conditions and image degradation from motion blur are considerable problems. In [4], the changes in the environment are not specifically considered when calculating the likelihood of alignment. Furthermore all landmarks are treated in the same manner. In our study, it is intended to construct a face tracking technique that works robustly even under severe conditions. To adapt to the changes in environment, the likelihood of alignment is calculated using various features that are robust for a particular situation. The PDM parameters, $\mathbf{p}$ in Eq. (2) are updated in the same manner as the conventional technique[4] using the estimated likelihood of alignment. Conclusively, tracking accuracy can be improved by changing the features and classifiers for different parts of the face.

3   Evaluation of the Likelihood of Alignment at a Particular Landmark Location

In this study, landmark locations are estimated using the likelihood maps and the accuracy of their positions is evaluated. The likelihood maps at each landmark location are generated according to Eq. (5). In Eq. (5) the classifier is generated using image features extracted at manually annotated landmark locations. The details of the local features and the classifier are described in the following sections.

3.1   Local Features

As features, the gray scaled patch, image gradient, Local Binary Patterns (LBP) [5], Local Directional Pattern (LDP) [6], Local Phase Quantization (LPQ) [7],

SIFT [8], SURF [9] and HOG [10] are used for producing response maps. The most important property of the LBP operator is its robustness to gray-scale changes caused by illumination variation. A LDP feature is obtained by computing the edge response values in all eight directions at each pixel position and generating a code from the magnitude of the relative strength. LPQ is based on quantizing the Fourier transform phase in the local neighborhood and is robust against the most common image blurs.

3.2   Classifiers

The positions of landmarks are estimated in the likelihood map as shown in Fig. 2. The likelihood in Eq. (5) is generated using a classifier C_i. Classifiers are generated using logistic regression and support vector machines (SVMs). Logistic regression is a type of probabilistic statistical classification model. An SVM model is a representation of the examples of points in space, mapped so that the examples of the categories are separated by a clear gap that is as wide as possible.

3.3   Facial Image Database Captured by a Mobile Camera

Facial images used in this study are captured by a camera embedded in Elfoid. This database includes images that have various facial expressions, lighting changes and partial occlusions. The subject changes its head pose considerably

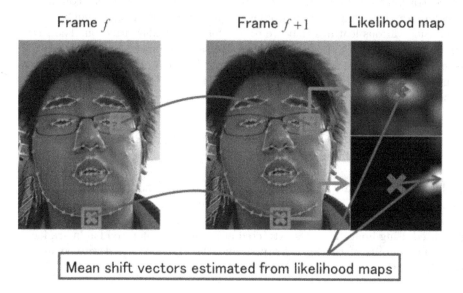

Fig. 2. The likelihood of alignment at a particular landmark location. Mean-shift vectors from each landmark are computed using the likelihood of alignment and the parameters **p** are updated.

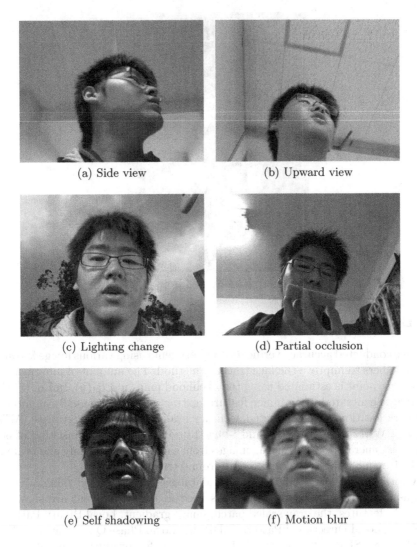

(a) Side view

(b) Upward view

(c) Lighting change

(d) Partial occlusion

(e) Self shadowing

(f) Motion blur

Fig. 3. Facial expressions captured in the strict environment

as do the conventional facial image databases such as AFW [11], LFPW [12], HELEN [13], and i-bug [14]. Furthermore, many blurred images are included because Elfoid is assumed to be used in the hand as a mobile phone. Facial images captured in strict environments are shown in Fig. 3. It is possible to find that various types of images, such as an upward view image and a blurred image which are not included in the conventional image database, are included in our database.

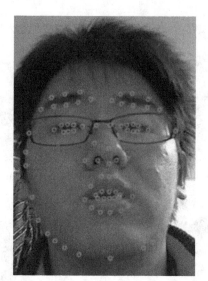

Fig. 4. Feature positions used in the experiment

4 Experiments

We have conducted accuracy verification experiments using various image features and classifiers to improve the face tracking method. The amount of movement of the feature point is estimated using the likelihood maps in Eq. (5). In Eq. (5) the classifier is generated using image features extracted at the manually annotated landmark locations. We conducted accuracy evaluations on our database, AFW [11], LFPW [12], HELEN [13], and i-bug [14]. This database, consisting of 500 images, is generated by extracting images from each database evenly and is annotated with an 83-point markup used as ground truth landmarks.

A total of 250 images, 50 from each database, were selected randomly and used as training data. Feature positions used in the experiment are shown in Fig. 4. As features, the gray scaled patch, image gradient, Local Binary Patterns (LBP) [5], Local Directional Pattern (LDP) [6], Local Phase Quantization (LPQ) [7], SIFT [8], SURF [9] and HOG [10] were used for producing the likelihood maps. Classifiers were generated using logistic regression and SVM. The size of the face region was normalized to 51x51 pixels. Image features were extracted at each feature position using 21x21 pixel regions. The size of the likelihood map was 11x11 pixels. The amount of movement of the feature point was estimated using the likelihood map generated from the results of the discrimination.

A total of 250 images that were not used as training data were used as test data. In the test phase, the Euclidean distance between the estimated position and the ground truth was used for an evaluation. As an evaluation of each facial part, Table 1 shows the number of optimal pairs of feature and classifier for discrimination. The results from Table 1 show that the optimal pairs of feature and classifier are different in each part of the face. To select the optimal feature and classifier by parts realizes accurate tracking.

Table 1. The number of optimal feature and classifier for discrimination in each part

feature	classifier	the number of features
Grayscale	Logistic regression	16
Grayscale	SVM	13
SURF	Logistic regression	12
SIFT	SVM	9
Gradient	Logistic regression	6
HOG	Logistic regression	6
SURF	SVM	6
HOG	SVM	4
LBP	SVM	3
LPQ	SVM	3
LDP	SVM	2
LBP	Logistic regression	1
LDP	Logistic regression	1
SIFT	Logistic regression	1
LPQ	Logistic regression	0
Gradient	SVM	0

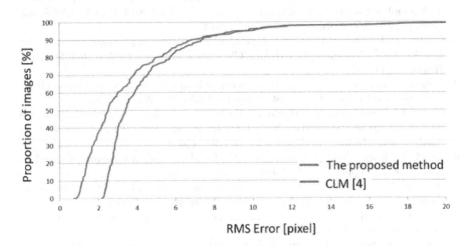

Fig. 5. Comparison between representative CLM [4] and the proposed method

We used the representative CLM [4] as the baseline method for comparison in this experiment. Figure 5 shows the comparison results. The proposed method used the combination of the features and classifiers in Table 1. The representative CLM [4] used image gradient and logistic regression. In Fig. 5, the horizontal axis shows RMS error and the vertical axis shows proportion of images. It can be seen that the proposed method outperforms the representative CLM [4].

5   Conclusions

We present local feature evaluations for the CLM framework. We conducted accuracy verification experiments using various image features and classifiers. In our study, tracking accuracy can be improved by changing the features and classifiers for different parts of the face. In future work, we will implement a face tracking system that can switch the features and classifiers adaptively, responding to changes in the environment.

Acknowledgments. This research was supported by the JST CREST (Core Research for Evolutional Science and Technology) research promotion program "Studies on cellphone-type teleoperated androids transmitting human presence."

References

1. Becker-Asano, C., Ogawa, K., Nishio, S., Ishiguro, H.: Exploring the uncanny valley with Geminoid HI-1 in a real-world application. In: Int'l Conf. Interfaces and Human Computer Interaction, pp. 121–128 (2010)
2. Tsuruda, Y., Hori, M., Yoshimura, H., Iwai, Y.: Generation of facial expression emphasized with cartoon techniques using a cellular-phone-type teleoperated robot with a mobile projector. In: Kurosu, M. (ed.) HCII/HCI 2013, Part V. LNCS, vol. 8008, pp. 391–400. Springer, Heidelberg (2013)
3. Cootes, T.F., Edwards, G.J., Taylor, C.J.: Active appearance models. In: Burkhardt, H., Neumann, B. (eds.) ECCV 1998. LNCS, vol. 1407, p. 484. Springer, Heidelberg (1998)
4. Saragih, J.M., Lucey, S., Cohn, J.F.: Deformable model fitting by regularized landmark mean-shift. Int'l Journal of Computer Vision **91**, 200–215 (2011)
5. Ojala, T., Pietikainen, M., Maenpaa, T.: Multiresolution gray scale and rotation invariant texture classification with local binary patterns. IEEE Trans. Pattern Analysis and Machine Intelligence **24**, 971–987 (2002)
6. Jabid, T., Kabir, M.H., Chae, O.: Robust facial expression recognition based on local directional pattern. ETRI Journal **32**(5) (2010)
7. Ahonen, T., Rahtu, E., Heikkila, J.: Recognition of blurred faces using local phase quantization. In: Int'l Conf. Pattern Recognition, pp. 1–4 (2008)
8. Lowe, D.G.: Object recognition from local scale-invariant features. Proc. Int'l Conf. Computer Vision **2**, 1150–1157 (1999)
9. Bay, H., Tuytelaars, T., Van Gool, L.: SURF: speeded up robust features. In: Leonardis, A., Bischof, H., Pinz, A. (eds.) ECCV 2006, Part I. LNCS, vol. 3951, pp. 404–417. Springer, Heidelberg (2006)
10. Dalal, N.: Histograms of oriented gradients for human detection. In: IEEE Conf. on Computer Vision and Pattern Recognition, pp. 886–893 (2005)
11. Zhu, X., Ramanan, D.: Face detection, pose estimation and landmark localization in the wild. In: IEEE Conf. on Computer Vision and Pattern Recognition, pp. 2879–2886 (2012)

12. Belhumeur, P.N., Jacobs, D.W., Kriegman, D.J., Kumar, N.: Localizing parts of faces using a consensus of exemplars. IEEE Trans. Pattern Analysis and Machine Intelligence **35**, 2930–2940 (2011)
13. Le, V., Brandt, J., Lin, Z., Bourdev, L., Huang, T.S.: Interactive facial feature localization. In: Fitzgibbon, A., Lazebnik, S., Perona, P., Sato, Y., Schmid, C. (eds.) ECCV 2012, Part III. LNCS, vol. 7574, pp. 679–692. Springer, Heidelberg (2012)
14. Sagonas, C., Tzimiropoulos, G., Zafeiriou, S., Pantic, M.: 300 faces in-the-wild challenge: The first facial landmark localization challenge. In: IEEE International Conference on Computer Vision (ICCV) Workshops (2013)

Multimodal Face Recognition for Profile Views Based on SIFT and LBP

Xiaona Xu[✉] and Yue Zhao

School of Information Engineering, Minzu University of China, Beijing 100081,
People's Republic of China
xu_xiaona@163.com

Abstract. This paper presents a multimodal face recognition system for profile views in such scenarios as frontal face images are not available. According to the special physiological location relationship and their supplement between face and ear, a framework of multimodal recognition system fusing profile-view face classifier and ear classifier is proposed. In profile-view face classifier, a new feature extraction and recognition algorithm based on Scale Invariant Feature Transform(SIFT)and local binary patterns (LBP) is applied. Firstly, a set of keypoints are extracted from the face image for matching by applying the SIFT algorithm; Secondly, each keypoint is described by the rotation-invariant LBP patterns; Finally, the matching pairs between the two sets of keypoints are determined by using the nearest neighbor distance ratio based matching strategy. Ear classifier is set up based on LDA. Then decision fusion of multimodal face recognition is carried out using the combination methods of Product, Sum, Median and Vote rules according to the Bayesian theory. The results of experiment show that our method improves the recognition performance and provides a new approach of non-intrusive recognition.

Keywords: Multimodal recognition · SIFT · LBP · Decision fusion

1 Introduction

Compared with other biometrics technologies, face recognition has turned out to be the focus of interest for a wide field of demanding applications in the last decades, due to its non-intrusive characteristics. A large number of face recognition methods have been proposed [1] and the reliable recognition of faces with slight variations in head pose and facial expression even for larger databases has nearly been reported [2]. However, most of these methods are designed to work with frontal face images. But in many cases, a frontal facial image is not available (e.g., the situation of a driver entering a gated area). In this paper we concentrate on the approach of face recognition for profile views.

Profile-view face recognition is confronted with several challenges: different poses, varying illumination, occlusion, and facial expressions. It is a feasible approach to fuse different kinds of data for a better decision. Earlier research has shown that human ear is one of the representative human biometrics with uniqueness and stability [3].

© Springer International Publishing Switzerland 2015
Q. Ji et al. (Eds.): FFER 2014, LNCS 8912, pp. 20–30, 2015.
DOI: 10.1007/978-3-319-13737-7_3

Because of ear's special physiological structure and location, it is reasonable to combine profile-view face with ear to make use of the supplement between ear and face biometrics, in such scenarios as frontal face images are not available. The fusion can fully utilize their connection relationship and increase the reliability of performance, especially provide an approach of non-intrusive authentication.

Scale Invariant Feature Transform (SIFT), proposed by D.G.Lowe in 1999 and improved in 2004, has been empirically proven to be one of the most robust among the local invariant feature descriptors with respect to different geometrical changes [4]. But SIFT feature could not solve the problems of expression, viewing angle and varying illumination very well due to its own boundedness in object recognition. The local binary pattern (LBP) operator is a texture descriptor that has been widely used in object recognition and achieved good performance in face recognition [5]. LBP possesses the merits of resistance to varying expression, viewing angle and illumination. So in this paper we investigate the feature extraction algorithm by combining SIFT and LBP features. The integrated SIFT-LBP descriptor in recognition is robust against the rotation, lighting, expression.

In this paper, we propose the multimodal face recognition method for profile views based on integrated SIFT-LBP features, and the result of experiments shows that our method improves the recognition performance and provides a new approach of non-intrusive recognition.

2   Feature Extraction and Classification Based on SIFT and LBP

2.1   Steps of Extracting SIFT Keypoints

SIFT, which is an efficient algorithm for object or scene recognition based on local 3D extrema in the scale-space pyramid built by difference-of Gaussian(DoG) filters, was proposed by Lowe in 1999 [4]. The steps of SIFT are as follows:

1. Scale-space extrema Detection

The scale space of an image is defined as a function $L(x, y, \sigma)$, that is produced from the convolution of a variable-scale Gaussian $G(x, y, \sigma)$, with an input image $I(x, y)$:

$$L(x, y, \sigma) = G(x, y, \sigma) * I(x, y) \tag{1}$$

To efficiently detect stable keypoint locations in scale space, it uses scale-space extrema in the DoG function convolved with the image $D(x, y, \sigma)$, which can be computed from the difference of two nearby scales separated by a constant multiplicative factor k:

$$D(x, y, \sigma) = (G(x, y, k\sigma) - G(x, y, \sigma)) * I(x, y)$$
$$= L(x, y, k\sigma) - L(x, y, \sigma)$$

(2)

In order to detect the local extrema of $D(x, y, \sigma)$, each sample point is compared to its eight neighbors in the current image and nine neighbors in the scale above and below. It is selected only if it is larger than all of these neighbors or smaller than all of them.

2. Keypoint localization

Once a keypoint candidate has been found by comparing a pixel to its neighbors, the next step is to perform a detailed fit to the nearby data for location, scale, and ratio of principal curvatures. This information allows points to be rejected that have low contrast and are therefore sensitive to noise or are poorly localized along and edge.

The principal curvatures can be computed from a 2×2 Hessian matrix, H, computed at the location and scale of the keypoint:

$$H = \begin{bmatrix} D_{xx} & D_{xy} \\ D_{xy} & D_{yy} \end{bmatrix}$$

(3)

where D is the differential of DoG space.
The stability is measured as follows:

$$\frac{(D_{xx} + D_{yy})^2}{D_{xx}D_{yy} - D_{xy}^2} < \frac{(r+1)^2}{r}$$

(4)

If the extrema could not satisfy the stability formula, it should be removed. r is the ratio of maximum eigenvalue to minimum eigenvalue, which is to control the stability of feature points.

3. Orientation assignment

For each image sample $L(x, y)$, at this scale, the gradient magnitude $m(x, y)$ and orientation $\theta(x, y)$ are computed using pixel differences:

$$m(x, y) = \sqrt{(L(x+1, y) - L(x-1, y))^2 + (L(x, y+1) - L(x, y-1))^2}$$
$$\theta(x, y) = \tan^{-1}((L(x, y+1) - L(x, y-1))/L(x+1, y) - L(x-1, y)))$$

(5)

So far, we get the information of location, scale and orientation of SIFT keypoints.

2.2   LBP Descriptor

LBP is a texture descriptive approach in gray-scale. It can be computed easily and used to describing the local features of an image effectively. It has good rotation invariance and illumination invariance, and has been successfully applied to face recognition.

The Original LBP Descriptor

The original LBP method is introduced by Ojala [6] to be used in texture description. It is based on thresholding neighborhood pixel values against the center pixel in a fixed 3×3 window in order to form a binary pattern. Then these LBP of different pixels are got through weighted sum as follows:

$$s\left(f_p - f_c\right) = \begin{cases} 1, f_p \geq f_c \\ 0, f_p < f_c \end{cases}$$

(6)

where f_c is the gray value corresponding to the local center pixel, and $f_p (p = 0,1,\cdots,7)$ corresponding to the eight neighborhood pixels.

Extending LBP Descriptor

We can use $LBP_{P,R}$ to denote LBP operators with different sizes, in which (P, R) means P sampling point on a circle of radius R. It allows for any value of P and R, for the gray values of neighbors which do not fall exactly in the center of pixels are estimated by bilinear interpolation.

$$LBP_{P,R} = \sum_{p=0}^{P-1} s\left(g_p - g_c\right) 2^p$$

(7)

Rotation-Invariant LBP

Rotation-invariant LBP can be achieved from $LBP_{P,R}$ through rotating operation as follows:

$$LBP_{P,R}^{ri} = \min(ROR(LBP_{P,R}, i))$$

(8)

2.3   Keypoint-Based Rotation-Invariant LBP Descriptor Vector

We define $p_i = (x, y, \sigma, \theta)$ as a keypoint detected by SIFT approach, where (x, y) is the location of pixel p_i in the original image, σ and θ is the scale and main direction of p_i respectively.

According to σ, we find the level of p_i in Gaussian Pyramid and get an image region of 15×15 around p_i. According to θ, we rotate the image region to referred orientation to enssure rotation-invariance. Then the 11×11 image region around p_i is selected as description region.

The steps of rotation-invariant LBP feature description are as follows:

Step 1: Choose a 9×9 region around p_i and compute the rotation- invariant pattern $LBP_{8,1}^{ri}$ around p_j respectively. These descriptors are composed as 81-dimension vector, i.e.: $LBP_j = [LBP_1, LBP_2, \cdots, LBP_{81}]$

Step 2: The farer is the distance of the pixel p_j to the center p_i, the smaller is the contribution of describing the information of p_i. Therefore LBP_j is weighted. The weight coefficient is defined as:

$$w_j = 1 / (\sqrt{(x_j - x_i)^2 + (y_j - y_i)^2} + 1) \tag{9}$$

where (x_i, x_j) and (y_i, y_j) are the coordinates of p_i and p_j respectively.

Step 3: The weighted LBP feature is computed as follows:

$$T_i = [w_1 \cdot LBP_1, w_2 \cdot LBP_2, \cdots, w_{81} \cdot LBP_{81}] \tag{10}$$

Step 4: In order to eliminate the influence of illumination variation, T_i is normalized:

$$\frac{T_i}{\|T_i\|} \to T_i \tag{11}$$

In the end, we get the 81-dimension descriptor T_i about the region around p_i. From the computing process, we can see that scale-invariance is acquired by using the scale of the keypoints, and rotation-invariance is acquired by rotating the image region to the referred orientation, and the robustness of illumination is acquired by the normalization of descriptor vector. Meanwhile, with the addition of the rotation-invariant LBP, which possesses certain scale, rotation and illumination invariance, the robustness of keypoint-based Rotation-invariant LBP descriptor vector is guaranteed.

2.4   Matching Method for Recognition

In this paper we adopt Euclidean distance as similarity measure between two keypoints. The best candidate matching for each keypoint is found by identifying its nearest neighbor in the database of keypoints from training images. Supposing T_A is one of the keypoints in the test image, T_B and T_C are the nearest neighbor point and the second-nearest neighbor point respectively matched in the train image, if the ratio of $\|T_A - T_B\|$ to $\|T_A - T_C\|$ is less that the threshold t, the keypoint A is thought to be matched with the nearest neighbor point B.

Then we use the similarity to measure the matching level of the two images I_t and I_r for recognition:

$$S = \frac{match(I_t, I_r)}{n_r} \tag{12}$$

where $match(I_t, I_r)$ is the amount of the valid matched descriptor vector with the method above, and n_r is the amount of keypoints detected in the given test image.

3   Multimodal Face Recognition for Profile Views

3.1   The Frame of Multimodal Recognition System

The unimodal recognition often confronts a variety of problems such as noisy data, intra-class variation, restricted degrees of freedom, non-universality, spoof attacks, and unacceptable error rates. Multimodal biometrics technology is becoming an important approach to alleviate these problems intrinsic to unimodal recognition systems [7]. Because of ear's special physiological structure and location, we propose to combine profile-view face classifier with ear classifier in such scenarios as frontal face images are not available to fully use their implement and increase the reliability of performance.

Information fusion in a biometric multimodal system can be performed at various levels: sensor level, feature level, opinion level and decision level [8]. In this paper we consider information fusing at the decision level. The frame of multimodal face recognition system based on profile views is showed in Fig. 1. The Profile face classifier extracts SIFT-LBP descriptor vector for matching and recognition. Since the ear images are cropped from profile-view face images, and SIFT-LBP descriptor gets the scale-based invariant feature, the ear classifier should get another feature descriptor for classification. In our system, ear classifier is established based on Full-Space Linear Discriminant Analysis. Then decision fusion of ear and profile face classifier is carried out using the combination methods according to the Bayesian theory.

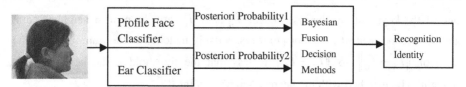

Fig. 1. The frame of multimodal recognition system based on profile views

3.2   The Estimation of Posterior Probability

To the given sample X_i, we firstly compute keypoint-based rotation-invariant LBP descriptor vector. Then we compute the similarity corresponding to the train samples. Here we estimate the posterior probability as follows:

$$P(X_i \mid R_j) = (1 / S_i^2) / \sum_{k=1}^{N} (1 / S_k^2) \qquad (13)$$

3.3   Fusion Method

During recognition, our goal is to evaluate the posterior probabilities of all multimodal classes given by an unknown input feature set. Here we adopt the combining classifiers methods based on the Bayesian theory [9]. Consider a pattern recognition problem where L different classifiers are applied and the recognition output of each classifier is $R_j (j = 1, 2, \cdots, L)$. The given sample X_i can and must be recognized as one class of N patterns. Let us assume that the prior probabilities of N patterns are equal. According to the Bayesian Theory, the given sample is recognized as the pattern n which has the highest posteriori probability as follows:

$$n = \arg(\max_{i=1,2,\cdots,N} P(X_i \mid R_1, R_2, \cdots, R_L)) \qquad (14)$$

Assume the recognition outputs of each classifier are independent, then we get the Product rule of combining multi-classifier is as follows:

$$n = \arg(\max_{i=1,2,\cdots,N} \prod_{j=1}^{L} P(X_i \mid R_j)) \qquad (15)$$

If we assume the posteriori probability $P(X_i \mid R_j)$ is changed near the prior probability $P(X_i)$, we can get the Sum rule:

$$n = \arg(\max_{i} \limits_{i=1,2,\cdots,N} \sum_{j=1}^{L} P(X_i \mid R_j)) \qquad (16)$$

Obviously, the Sum rule is actually based on the average, and the better estimate of the average is the median. So the Median rule of combining classifiers is as follows:

$$n = \arg(\max_{i} \limits_{i=1,2,\cdots,N} (\underset{j=1,2,\cdots,L}{med} P(X_i \mid R_j)) \qquad (17)$$

If we binarize the posterior probability, we can get the Vote rule of combining multi-classifiers. But the general Vote rule is not suitable to the problem with only two classifiers in our system. This is because, if both of the two classifiers assign the given sample to the different classes, the votes appear equal so that the system cannot make a decision. So the general Vote rule need be modified to avoid this problem. In each classifier, we add the second candidate to the first candidate. Here we assume the second candidate as $\beta\alpha_j, 0 < \beta < 1$, and add the first candidate votes and so its weight changes to be $(\alpha_j + (P_1 - P_2))$, where α_j is the weight of the i th classifier, P_1 and P_2 are the first and second highest posterior probability which the classifier gives. The modified is reasonable because if $(P_1 - P_2)$ is low, we should increase the weight of the second candidate but it cannot be beyond the first candidate. Then the modified Vote rule is as follows:

$$k_{j1} = \arg(\max_{i} \limits_{i=1,2,\cdots,N} (P(X_i \mid R_j)))$$

$$k_{j2} = \arg(\max_{i} \limits_{\substack{i=1,2,\cdots,N \\ i \neq k_{j1}}} (P(X_i \mid R_j)))$$

$$vote_{kj} = \begin{cases} \alpha_j + (P_1 - P_2), k = k_{j1} \\ \beta\alpha_j, k = k_{j2} \\ 0, otherwise \end{cases}$$

$$n = \arg(\max_{i} \limits_{i=1,2,\cdots,N} (\sum_{j=1}^{L} vote_{ij})) \qquad (18)$$

4   Experiments and Results

We use the multimodal image database from USTB [10]. It consists of multi-view face images of 79 persons with variations of the head position and slight facial expressions, and some persons wear glasses. Define the rotation degree of profile-view face image as 0°. We select 7 images including the rotation from -30° to +30° with 10° interval for our experiments.

Before performing multimodal recognition based on profile-view face which fuses face and ear feature, input images should be preprocessed and normalized. First pure ear images in the profile-view face images are cropped. Fig.2 gives one example of cropped profile-view face and ear gray images. In the experiments, the former 5 images per person are used as the gallery and the other 2 images are used as the probe.

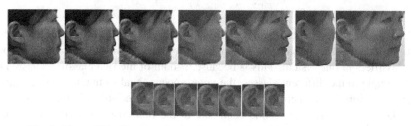

Fig. 2. Cropped Profile-view face and ear gray-image example for one person

4.1   Comparison of Different Recognition Methods

First we compare the SIFT-LBP algorithm in this paper with other face recognition algorithm. The experiment result is shown in Table 1.

Table 1. Comparison of Different Recognition Methods

Algorithm	Recognition Rate (Profile-view face)
FSLDA	87.97 %
SIFT	82.91%
SIFT-LBP	94.93%

4.2   Speed Analysis of the SIFT-LBP Feature Extraction Algorithm

In our algorithm the feature descriptor of the keypoint is reduced to 81-dimension from 128-dimension of the standard SIFT algorithm, so the matching speed of keypoints is improved well. The experiment result is shown in Table 2.

Table 2. Comparison of the Algorithm Speed

	Time (s)	Gaussian Factor σ
SIFT	2.2	0.03
SIFT-LBP	1.58	0.05

4.3   Performance of Multimodal Recognition

To verify the performance of multimodal recognition, we compare it with the performance of profile-view or ear face unimodal recognition. The results are shown in Table 3.

Table 3. Experimental Results of Multimodal and Unimodal Recognition

Fusion Scheme	Recognition Rate		
	Profile-view face (SIFT-LBP)	Ear (LDA)	Multimodal Recognition
No combination	94.93 %	93.67 %	
Product rule			96.20 %
Sum rule			98.10 %
Median rule			98.10 %
Modified Vote rule			97.47 %

5   Conclusion

In this paper, in such cases as a frontal facial image is not available, we propose a novel multimodal recognition based on profile-view face images on decision level fusion for non-intrusive authentication. In profile-view face classifier, a new feature extraction and recognition algorithm based on Scale Invariant Feature Transform (SIFT) and local binary patterns (LBP) is applied. Ear classifier is set up based on LDA. Finally decision fusion of ear and profile face is carried out using the combination methods of product, sum and median rules according to the Bayesian theory. The result of experiment shows that the recognition rate is higher than that of the recognition adopting the single features. The work provides a new effective approach of non-intrusive biometric recognition.

Acknowledgements. This work is supported by the first-class university and first-rate discipline funds of Minzu University of China and by the Fundamental Research Funds for the Central Universities.

References

1. Zhao, W., Chellappa, R., Phillips, P., Rosenfeld, A.: Face recognition: A literature survey. ACM Computing Surveys, pp. 399–458 (2003)
2. Phillips, P.J., Scruggs, T.: Overview of the face recognition grand challenge. In: Proc. of IEEE Computer Society Conference on Computer Vision and Pattern Recognition, pp. 947–954, San Diego, USA (2005)
3. Yuan, L., Mu, Z., Liu, K.: Personal Recognition with ear biometrics. Pattern Recognition and Artificial Intelligence 18(3), 310–315 (2005). (in Chinese)
4. Lowe, D.G.: Distinctive image features from scale-invariant keypoints. International Journal of Computer Vision 60(2), 91–110 (2004)
5. Ahonen, T., Hadid, A., Pietikäinen, M.: Face recognition with local binary patterns. In: Pajdla, T., Matas, J. (eds.) ECCV 2004. LNCS, vol. 3021, pp. 469–481. Springer, Heidelberg (2004)

6. Ojala, T., Pietikainen, M., Harwood, D.: A comparative study of texture measures with classification based on feature distributions. Pattern Recognition **29**(1), 51–59 (1996)
7. Ross, A., Jain, A.: Multimodal biometrics: an overview. In: Proc. of 12th European Processing Conference, pp. 1221–1224 (2004)
8. Faundez-Zanuy, M.: Data fusion in biometrics. Aerospace and Electronic Systems Magazine **20**(1), 34–38 (2005)
9. Dong, H.-M., Gao, J., Wang, R.-G.: Fusion of Multiple Classifiers for Face Recognition and Person Authentication. Journal of System Simulation **16**(8), 1849–1853 (2004). (in Chinese)
10. http://www.ustb.edu.cn/resb/

Face Alignment and Facial Expression Recognition

Learning the Face Shape Models
for Facial Landmark Detection in the Wild

Yue Wu and Qiang Ji[✉]

Department of ECSE, Rensselaer Polytechnic Institute, Troy, NY 12180, USA
{wuy9,jiq}@rpi.edu

Abstract. Facial landmark detection in the wild is challenging due to the appearance and shape variations caused by facial expressions, head poses, illuminations, and occlusions. To tackle this problem, we propose two probabilistic face shape models that could capture the face shape variations in different conditions. The first model is a undirected graphical model constructed based on the Restricted Boltzmann Machine (RBM). It decouples the shape variations into expression related and pose related parts. The second model is a directed hierarchical probabilistic model that specifically uses the head pose and expression labels in model construction. It embeds the local shape variations for each facial component, and automatically exploits the relationships among facial components, expressions and head poses. Experiments on benchmark databases show the effectiveness of the proposed probabilistic face shape models for facial landmark detection in the wild.

Keywords: Facial landmark detection · Face shape model · Restricted Boltzmann Machine · Hierarchial probabilistic model

1 Introduction

Face analysis is curial for human and computer interaction, since it provides useful information about human emotions, eye gaze directions, identity information and so on. In the task of face analysis, facial landmark detection plays an important role. It detects and localizes the facial key points such as eye corners, eyebrow tips on facial image (landmarks shown in Figure 1). Based on the detected facial landmark locations, algorithms could be applied to estimate the head poses [1], recognize the facial expressions [2], and verify human identities.

Facial landmark detection is challenging on "in-the-wild" facial images, since the facial appearance and shape (spatial relationships among landmarks) vary with facial expressions, head poses, illuminations and occlusions. For example, as shown in Figure 1, with different facial expressions and head poses, the facial appearance and shape change dramatically. Illumination will cause the change of the facial appearance. Part of the face would be occluded by other objects. To tackle those difficulties, the existing works usually propose sophisticated algorithms to model the appearance and shape variations.

© Springer International Publishing Switzerland 2015
Q. Ji et al. (Eds.): FFER 2014, LNCS 8912, pp. 33–45, 2015.
DOI: 10.1007/978-3-319-13737-7_4

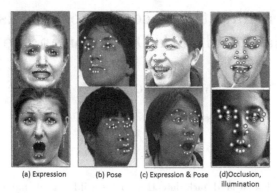

Fig. 1. Facial landmark detection on images with different variations. Images are from (a) CK+ [5], (b) FERET [6], (c) ISL [7], (d) AFLW [8] databases described in section 5.1.

In this paper, we focus on the modeling of face shape variations in difficult conditions for facial landmark detection in the wild. Specifically, we propose two probabilistic graphical models [3] [4] to capture the face shape patterns and their variations across varying facial expressions, head poses, etc. The first model is constructed based on the Restricted Boltzmann Machine (RBM). The second model is a hierarchical probabilistic graphical model. Comparing to the first model, the second model explicitly adds the pose and expression labels to help the learning. In the probabilistic graphical model point of view, the first model is a undirected model, while the second one is a directed model.

The remaining parts of the paper are organized as follows: In section 2, we review the related research work. In section 3 and 4, we introduce the two proposed models, respectively. We discuss the experiments in section 5 and conclude this paper in section 6.

2   Related Work

Facial landmark detection algorithms can be classified into two major categories: holistic methods and constrained local methods (CLM).

Holistic Method: The holistic methods build models to capture the facial appearance and shape of the whole face. Typical holistic methods are Active Shape Model (ASM) [9] and Active Appearance Model (AAM) [10]. The ASM is a linear generative model that captures the face shape variations using Principle Component Analysis techniques. AAM models both the appearance and shape variations to fit a linear generative model.

Constrained Local Methods (CLM): Typical local methods model the local image appearances of each facial landmark independently, and build complex face shape models to constrain the shape variations among facial landmarks. The early work is proposed by Cristinacce and Cootes [11]. They build template model for local appearance and use ASM as the global shape constraint. In [12], Valstar et al. propose method to combine the Boosted Regression and Markov Networks (BoRMaN) for facial landmark detection. It generates the likelihood map for each point based on the response of the support vector regressor, and then constraints the point locations by the shape distribution embedded in a pre-trained Markov Network model. Based on [12], Martinez et al. [13] propose a Local Evidence Aggregation for Regression (LEAR) based facial feature detection method to further improve the local point searching procedure by considering the aggregation of local evidence. More recently, there are works focus on the in-the-wild images. For example, to detect landmarks on images with large head pose variations, Zhu and Ramanan [14] propose the joint Face Detection, Pose Estimation, and Landmark Localization (FPLL) method. In their algorithm, they build pose-dependent deformable part model with tree structure during training, and maximize over different poses during testing.

More recently, there are works that formulate facial landmark detection as a regression problem. For example, in [15], face alignment is formulated as a nonlinear lease-square problem, and supervised descent method is used to predict the displacement vectors to fit the facial image. Please refer to [3][4] for more detailed discussions about other related works.

In this paper, our works follow the constrained local method and we propose two face shape models [3][4] for facial landmark detection in the wild. Our models differ from the existing face shape models proposed in the previous works [9][12][13][14]. First, we explicitly consider the face shape variations due to both facial expression and head pose changes. Second, unlike the previous works, our models do not need to estimate the head pose or maximize over different head poses [14] in testing. Instead, the proposed models treat the pose as hidden variable and the models can marginalize over it. Third, the proposed models are higher order models considering the global shape variations among points. This is better than the model in [12][13][14] where only the shape constraints of local pairwise points are considered. In the following two sections, we discuss two models in details.

3   Model I: RBM Based Face Shape Model for Facial Landmark Detection

The first face shape model is constructed based on the Restricted Boltzmann Machine and its variants. In the following, we first introduce the model and discuss how to use it for facial landmark detection.

3.1   RBM Based Face Shape Model

Face shapes tend to change with facial expressions and head poses on in-the-wild images. Modeling these complex variations in the high dimensional space is challenging. However, we could decouple the variations into facial expression related part and pose related part. Based on this intuition, we proposed the RBM based

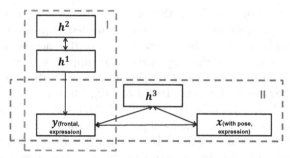

Part I: Frontal face shape prior Part II: Transfer to
with different expressions   different poses

Fig. 2. Face shape prior model (model I) based on the combination of the DBNs and 3-way RBM

model shown in Figure 2. In the model, variable $\mathbf{x} = \{x_1, x_2, ...\}$ represents the coordinates of the facial landmark locations where face could be in arbitrary facial expressions and poses. Variable $\mathbf{y} = \{y_1, y_2, ...\}$ represents the corresponding facial landmark locations of $\mathbf{x}$ with frontal head pose. There are three sets of hidden nodes, including $\mathbf{h}^1$, $\mathbf{h}^2$, and $\mathbf{h}^3$. The model contains two parts. In the first part, nodes $\mathbf{y}$, $\mathbf{h}^1$, and $\mathbf{h}^2$ form a Deep Belief Networks (DBN) [16] that could captures the face shape variations due to facial expression changes. In the second part, nodes $\mathbf{x}$, $\mathbf{y}$, and $\mathbf{h}^3$ form a factored 3-way Restricted Boltzmann Machine model [17] that captures the transition from frontal face shapes with expressions to face shapes with arbitrary poses and same expressions. With both part I and II, the proposed model decomposes the shape variations into expression and pose related parts, and captures the joint variations in the unified framework. In the following, we further discuss each part separately.

In part I, the Deep Belief Network (DBN) model [16] consists of three layers. The consecutive layers are modeled using the Restrictive Boltzmann Machine model (RBM). For example, considering the bottom two layers, the RBM models the probabilistic density function of the observed variable $\mathbf{y}$ as:

$$p_\eta(\mathbf{y}) = \frac{1}{Z} \sum_{\mathbf{h}^1} e^{-E_\eta(\mathbf{y}, \mathbf{h}^1)}, \tag{1}$$

where $Z = \sum_{\mathbf{y}, \mathbf{h}^1} e^{-E_\eta(\mathbf{y}, \mathbf{h}^1)}$ is the partition function, and $\mathbf{h}^1 \in \{0, 1\}^{\mathcal{H}}$ represents binary hidden variables. The probability is defined in terms of the joint energy function over $\mathbf{y}$ and $\mathbf{h}^1$, as:

$$-E_\eta(\mathbf{y}, \mathbf{h}^1) = \sum_i \mathbf{b}_i \mathbf{y}_i + \sum_{i,j} \mathbf{W}_{ij}^1 \mathbf{y}_i \mathbf{h}_j^1 + \sum_j \mathbf{c}_j \mathbf{h}_j^1, \tag{2}$$

where $\mathbf{W}_{ij}^1$ is the interaction strength between the hidden node $\mathbf{h}_j^1$ and the visible node $\mathbf{y}_i$. $\mathbf{b}$ and $\mathbf{c}$ are the biases for the visible layer and hidden layer. The parameters in this model, $(\mathbf{W}^1, \mathbf{c}, \mathbf{b})$, are collectively represented as η. During training, each set of RBM parameters (for layer 1&2 and 2&3) are pre-trained in a layer-wise manner by maximizing the log likelihood using Contrastive Divergence algorithm [18], for the sake of the learning efficiency. The model is then fine-tuned jointly [16].

In part II, the factored 3-way RBM model [17] captures the transition from frontal face shapes with expression ($\mathbf{y}$) to face shapes with arbitrary poses and the same expression ($\mathbf{x}$). The joint energy function of the factorized 3-way RBM model can be written as (ignoring the bias terms):

$$- E_\theta(\mathbf{x}, \mathbf{y}, \mathbf{h}^3) = \sum_f (\sum_i \mathbf{x}_i \mathbf{W}_{if}^x)(\sum_j \mathbf{y}_j \mathbf{W}_{jf}^y)(\sum_k \mathbf{h}_k^3 \mathbf{W}_{kf}^h), \qquad (3)$$

where the parameters $\theta = \{\mathbf{W}_{if}^x, \mathbf{W}_{jf}^y, \mathbf{W}_{kf}^h\}$ describe the interactions among variables. Then, the model captures the joint probability of $\mathbf{x}$ and $\mathbf{y}$ as follows:

$$p_\theta(\mathbf{x}, \mathbf{y}) = \frac{1}{Z} \sum_{\mathbf{h}^3} e^{-E_\theta(\mathbf{x}, \mathbf{y}, \mathbf{h}^3)}, \qquad (4)$$

where $Z = \sum_{\mathbf{x}, \mathbf{y}, \mathbf{h}^3} e^{-E_\theta(\mathbf{x}, \mathbf{y}, \mathbf{h}^3)}$ is the partition function. Given the pairwise training data $\{\mathbf{x}_i, \mathbf{y}_i\}_{i=1}^N$, parameter learning are performed by maximizing the log joint likelihood using the Contrastive Divergence algorithm [18]. For detailed discussion about the learning algorithm, please refer to [3].

3.2 Facial Landmark Detection Using the RBM Based Face Shape Model

Facial landmark detection accuracy and robustness can be improved by incorporating the proposed face shape prior model. Assume that we construct the local facial landmark detectors using Support Vector Machine [19] based on the local image patch, and detect landmark following the scanning window manner, we can generate the initial measurements of the facial landmark locations $\mathbf{m} = \{m_1, m_2, ...\}$. Our goal is to estimate the true facial landmark locations $\mathbf{x}$ through the probabilistic inference:

$$\mathbf{x}^* = \arg\max_{\mathbf{x}} P(\mathbf{x}|\mathbf{m}) = \arg\max_{\mathbf{x}} P(\mathbf{m}|\mathbf{x}) P(\mathbf{x}) \qquad (5)$$

Here, $p(\mathbf{m}|\mathbf{x})$ is modeled by the multivariate Gaussian distribution. It is difficult to analytically formulate the prior probability $p(\mathbf{x})$ from the learned model described in section 3.1. We hence propose to estimate the local prior probability numerically via sampling using the learned model. Please refer to [3] for the detailed discussion about sample generation. Given the generated samples, we could further estimate the local prior distribution $p(\mathbf{x})$ with Gaussian assumption . We then combine the prior and likelihood to infer the facial landmark location for detection.

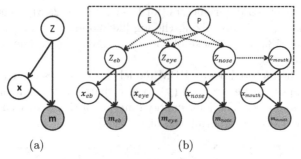

(a)   (b)

Fig. 3. Hierarchical Probabilistic Model. (a) Component model. (b) A sample structure. Node connections marked as solid lines are fixed while these with dotted lines are learned.

4   Model II: A Hierarchical Probabilistic Face Shape Model for Facial Landmark Detection

The second face shape model is a directed hierarchical probabilistic graphical model. Unlike model I in section 3, for this model, we specifically add the head pose and facial expression labels for model construction. By adding this information, we aim to capture the shape variations of each facial component, and automatically exploit the relationships among facial components, the facial expressions and the poses. In the following, we first discuss the model, its training and inference. We then discuss how to use the model for facial landmark detection.

4.1   A Hierarchical Probabilistic Face Shape Model

As shown in Figure 3 (b), our hierarchical model consists of nodes from four layers. Nodes in the bottom layer indicate the measurements of facial feature locations generated using the local point detectors for each facial component, denoted as $\mathbf{m}_{eyebrow}$, $\mathbf{m}_{eye}$, $\mathbf{m}_{nose}$, and $\mathbf{m}_{mouth}$. Nodes in the second layer represent the true facial feature locations we want to infer, denoted as $\mathbf{x}_{eyebrow}$, $\mathbf{x}_{eye}$, $\mathbf{x}_{nose}$, and $\mathbf{x}_{mouth}$. In the third layer, all nodes are discrete latent random variables indicating the states of each facial component. The top layer contains two discrete nodes E and P representing the facial expression and the pose.

This model captures two levels of information. The lower level information refers to the local shape variations of each facial component embedding in the lower three layers of nodes, belonging to the same facial component. The higher level information is the joint relationships among facial components, facial expressions, and head poses represented by the connections of nodes within the rectangle in Figure 3 (b).

For the lower level information of local shape variations (Figure 3 (a)), we model it by the Gaussian mixture model as follows:

$$P(\mathbf{x}, \mathbf{m}) = \sum_Z P(\mathbf{m}|\mathbf{x}, Z)P(\mathbf{x}|Z)P(Z), \tag{6}$$

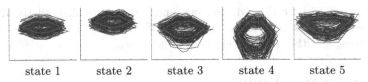

state 1   state 2   state 3   state 4   state 5

Fig. 4. Examples of the shape variations of the mouth for different hidden states. Learned from data with expression variations.

where $P(\mathbf{x}|Z = z)$ is a multivariate Gaussian distribution and $P(\mathbf{m}|\mathbf{x}, Z = z)$ is a linear multivariate Gaussian distribution. $P(Z)$ is the probability for different hidden states. Figure 4 shows the shape variations of mouth learned from data with facial expression variations.

For the higher level information about the relationships among facial components, expressions and poses, we propose to learn them through automatic parameter and structure learning, since those relationships should not be assigned manually and arbitrarily. Here, the dotted lines within the rectangle in Figure 3 (b) are shown as a special example for illustration purposes only.

With the combination of local shape models for each facial component, and the global relationship among facial components, facial expressions and poses, the overall joint probability of $\mathbf{x}$ and $\mathbf{m}$ is formulated as:

$$P(\mathbf{x}, \mathbf{m}) = \sum_{Z,E,P} (\prod_{i \in \{eb,e,n,m\}} P(\mathbf{m}_{,i}, \mathbf{x}_i | Z_i)) P(Z, E, P), \tag{7}$$

where $Z = [Z_{eb}, Z_e, Z_n, Z_m]$.

4.2 Model Learning

Given the true feature location $\mathbf{x}$, its measurement $\mathbf{m}$, its facial expression label E, and pose label P as training data, we could learn the model. Here, the measurements are generated using the local point detector similarly as illustrated in section 3.2. We refer to model learning as learning the model structure and the model parameters. As shown in Figure 3(b), for structure learning, we only learn the global structure, denoted as $\mathbf{M}_G$ that connects the nodes within the rectangular block, and we fix the local model $\mathbf{M}_L$. For parameter learning, we estimate the parameters of the whole model $\Theta = [\Theta_G, \Theta_L]$. The learning is difficult, due to the existence of hidden nodes Z. To tackle this learning task, we applied the Structure EM algorithm [20] and modified it for our application. For details, please refer to [4].

4.3 Inference Though the Model for Facial Landmark Detection

Assume that we generate the initial measurements of facial landmark locations $\mathbf{m}$ using the local point detectors. We could perform facial landmark detection through inference in the proposed hierarchical model:

$$\mathbf{x}^* = \arg\max_{\mathbf{x}} P(\mathbf{x}|\mathbf{m}) \tag{8}$$

It is important to note that, during inference, we marginalize all the discrete latent states Z_i, unknown facial expression E and pose P. Here we use the junction tree algorithm [21] to perform the inference.

5   Experimental Results

In this section, we test the proposed two facial landmark detection algorithms on several benchmark databases with different variations.

5.1   Implementation Details

Databases: Both algorithms are tested on five benchmark databases with different variations as shown in Table 1 and Figure 7. Specifically, the Extended Cohn-Kanade AU-coded Expression (CK+) database [5] and MMI Facial expression (MMI) database [22] contain facial image sequences with 6 basic facial expressions, including anger, disgust, fear, happiness, sadness and surprised. For each sequence, we used the first frame, onset and apex frames. In total, CK+ contains 1339 images and MMI contains 584 images. The Facial Recognition Technology (FERET) database [6] contains facial images with different poses and we used 335 frontal, quarter left and right images. The Intelligent Systems Lab (ISL) multi-view facial expression database [7] contains sequences of 8 subjects showing happy and surprised facial expressions under varying continuous head poses. We selected about every 5 frames and some key frames from each sequence. In total, there are 460 images in our experiments. The Annotated Facial Landmarks in the Wild (AFLW) database [8] contains images collected from the website with large appearance and shape variations. In our experiments, we used 4226 images for which all the annotations of the inner points are available. For each database, we used cross-validation strategy to test the proposed algorithms.

Table 1. Benchmark databases and the encoded variations

Variations	expression	pose	expression + pose
Databases	CK+ [5] MMI [22]	FERET [6] AFLW [8]	ISL [7]

Measurements: The distance error metric is defined as below:

$$error = \frac{\|\mathbf{x} - \hat{\mathbf{x}}\|_2}{\|\mathbf{x}_{le} - \mathbf{x}_{re}\|_2}, \tag{9}$$

where $\mathbf{x}$ and $\hat{\mathbf{x}}$ represent the ground truth and detected facial landmark locations. $\mathbf{x}_{le}$ and $\mathbf{x}_{re}$ represent the ground truth locations of the left and right eyes.

5.2   Experimental Results on CK+ Database

In this subsection, we discuss the performances of the two proposed models on CK+ databases, respectively. In the next subsections, we compare them to the state-of-the-art on all databases.

Model I. As shown in Table 2, by using the proposed RBM based face shape model (Model I), the overall facial landmark detection error decreases by 16.88%. Figure 5 shows that the proposed RBM based face shape model decreases the detection errors for images with all facial expressions and the performances are similar.

Table 2. Facial landmark detection errors on CK+ database using RBM based face shape model (Model I)

	Eyebrow	Eye	Nose	Mouth	Overall
Initial measurements	8.7367	4.5367	7.7240	3.9704	5.8220
Proposed method (Model I)	7.4111	3.6214	5.2871	3.9046	4.8394

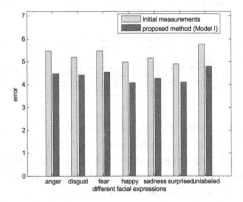

Fig. 5. Facial landmark detection errors for different facial expressions on CK+ database using the proposed RBM based face shape model (Model I)

Model II. We learn the hierarchical probabilistic model (Model II) on CK+ database, and its structure is shown in 6 (a). As can be seen, only the eyebrow and mouth directly link to the expression node. Eye and nose are independent of expression given the states of mouth. The learned local shape variations of the mouth have been shown in Figure 4, and the learned states are highly related to different facial expressions.

The overall facial feature detection accuracy on the CK+ database is shown in Table 3. With the learned hierarchical model, performance is better than the manually constructed model without the hidden states shown in Figure 6 (b).

5.3 Experimental Comparisons on Other Databases

In this subsection, we show the facial landmark detection performances using the two proposed face shape models on benchmark databases with difference variations, and compare them to the state-of-the-art works, including the BoRMaN

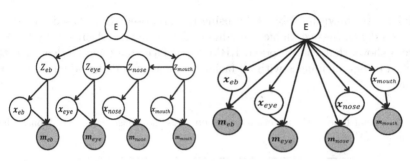

(a) Learned model structure

(b) Manually constructed model structure without hidden nodes

Fig. 6. Hierarchical model for CK+ database (Model II)

Table 3. Detection results using learned and manually constructed models on CK+ database (Model II)

	Eyebrow	Eye	Nose	Mouth	Overall
Initial measurements	8.7367	4.5367	7.7240	3.9704	5.8220
Manual	5.5487	3.0357	5.3267	3.8645	4.2233
Learned	5.4287	2.8466	4.8856	3.8212	4.0560

model [12], the LEAR model [13], the FPLL model [14], and the Supervised Descent method [15]. Please refer to section 2 for the discussions of those works.

The facial landmark detection results are shown in Table 4, Figure 7 and Figure 8. We see that the hierarchical probabilistic face shape model (model II) is slightly better than the RBM based face shape model (model I) on all databases. Both algorithms are better than the BoRMaN, LEAR and FPLL algorithms on all databases. The proposed algorithms are slightly worse than the supervised descent method on AFLW database.

Table 4. Facial landmark detection errors of different algorithms on CK+, MMI, FERET, and ISL databases. Numbers with "*" are the reported results in original papers.

| | Expression | | Pose | Exp.& pose |
	CK+	MMI	FERET	ISL
RBM model I	4.84	5.53	9.35	6.78
Hierarchical model II	4.05	5.04	6.91	6.77
BoRMaN [12]	6.94	6.64 (4.65*)	12.73	fails
LEAR [13]	9.27	6.24 (5.12*)	9.24	fails
FPLL [14]	8.76	8.34	9.3	fails

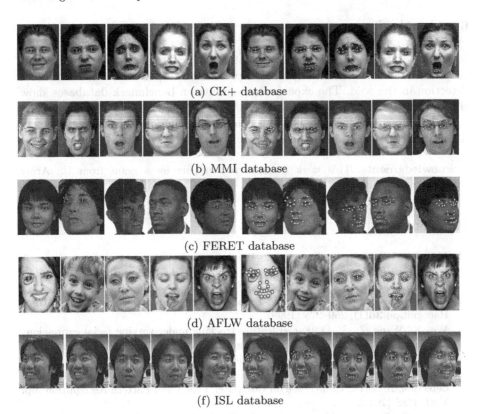

(a) CK+ database

(b) MMI database

(c) FERET database

(d) AFLW database

(f) ISL database

Fig. 7. Facial landmark detection results using the proposed face shape models on sample images from different databases. Left column: RBM based model I. Right column: Hierarchical model II. (Better see in color).

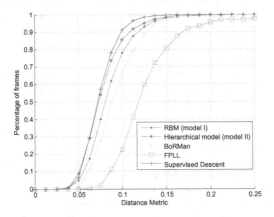

Fig. 8. Cumulative distribution curves of different algorithms on AFLW database. x axis: error threshold. y axis: percentages of images on which the errors are less than the thresholds.

6 Conclusion

In this paper, we proposed two probabilistic graphical models to capture the face shape variations under varying facial expressions and poses for facial landmark detection in the wild. The experimental results on benchmark databases show the effectiveness of the proposed models. In the future, we would extend those models to consider more challenging conditions, such as extreme poses where some points are not visible, and occlusions.

Acknowledgments. This work is supported in part by a grant from US Army Research office (W911NF-12-C-0017).

References

1. Murphy-Chutorian, E., Trivedi, M.: Head pose estimation in computer vision: A survey. IEEE Transactions on Pattern Analysis and Machine Intelligence **31**(4), 607–626 (2009)
2. Fasel, B., Luettin, J.: Automatic facial expression analysis: A survey. Pattern Recognition **36**(1), 259–275 (1999)
3. Wu, Y., Wang, Z., Ji, Q.: Facial feature tracking under varying facial expressions and face poses based on restricted boltzmann machines. In: IEEE Conference on Computer Vision and Pattern Recognition, pp. 3452–3459 (2013)
4. Wu, Y., Wang, Z., Ji, Q.: A hierarchical probabilistic model for facial feature detection. In: IEEE Conference on Computer Vision and Pattern Recognition, pp. 1781–1788 (2014)
5. Lucey, P., Cohn, J., Kanade, T., Saragih, J., Ambadar, Z., Matthews, I.: The extended cohn-kanade dataset (ck+): a complete dataset for action unit and emotion-specified expression. In: 2010 IEEE Computer Society Conference on Computer Vision and Pattern Recognition Workshops (CVPRW), pp. 94–101 (2010)
6. Phillips, P., Moon, H., Rauss, P., Rizvi, S.: The feret evaluation methodology for face-recognition algorithms. In: IEEE Conference on Computer Vision and Pattern Recognition, pp. 137–143 (1997)
7. Tong, Y., Liao, W., Ji, Q.: Isl multi-view facial expression database. http://www.ecse.rpi.edu/cvrl/database/database.html
8. Koestinger, M., Wohlhart, P., Roth, P.M., Bischof, H.: Annotated facial landmarks in the wild: a large-scale, real-world database for facial landmark localization. In: First IEEE International Workshop on Benchmarking Facial Image Analysis Technologies (2011)
9. Cootes, T.F., Taylor, C.J., Cooper, D.H., Graham, J.: Active shape models their training and application. Comput. Vis. Image Underst. **61**(1), 38–59 (1995)
10. Cootes, T.F., Edwards, G.J., Taylor, C.J.: Active appearance models. IEEE Transactions on Pattern Analysis and Machine Intelligence **23**(6), 681–685 (2001)
11. Cristinacce, D., Cootes, T.: Automatic feature localisation with constrained local models. Pattern Recognition **41**(10), 3054–3067 (2008)
12. Valstar, M., Martinez, B., Binefa, V., Pantic, M.: Facial point detection using boosted regression and graph models. In: IEEE International Conference on Computer Vision and Pattern Recognition, pp. 13–18 (2010)

13. Martinez, B., Valstar, M.F., Binefa, X., Pantic, M.: Local evidence aggregation for regression-based facial point detection. IEEE Transactions on Pattern Analysis and Machine Intelligence **35**(5), 1149–1163 (2013)
14. Zhu, X., Ramanan, D.: Face detection, pose estimation, and landmark localization in the wild. In: IEEE International Conference on Computer Vision and Pattern Recognition, pp. 2879–2886 (2012)
15. Xiong, X., De la Torre Frade, F.: Supervised descent method and its applications to face alignment. In: IEEE International Conference on Computer Vision and Pattern Recognition (CVPR), May 2013
16. Hinton, G.E., Osindero, S.: A fast learning algorithm for deep belief nets. Neural Computation **18**, 1527–1554 (2006)
17. Ranzato, M., Krizhevsky, A., Hinton, G.E.: Factored 3-way restricted boltzmann machines for modeling natural images. Journal of Machine Learning Research **9**, 621–628 (2010)
18. Hinton, G.E.: Training products of experts by minimizing contrastive divergence. Neural Comput. **14**(8), 1771–1800 (2002)
19. Fan, R.-E., Chang, K.-W., Hsieh, C.-J., Wang, X.-R., Lin, C.-J.: LIBLINEAR: A library for large linear classification. Journal of Machine Learning Research **9**, 1871–1874 (2008)
20. Friedman, N.: Learning belief networks in the presence of missing values and hidden variables. In: International Conference on Machine Learning, pp. 125–133. Morgan Kaufmann (1997)
21. Koller, D., Friedman, N.: Probabilistic Graphical Models: Principles and Techniques. MIT Press (2009)
22. Pantic, M., Valstar, M., Rademaker, R., Maat, L.: Web-based database for facial expression analysis. In: IEEE International Conference on Multimedia and Expo, ICME 2005, pp. 317–321 (2005)

Multimodal Facial Expression Recognition Based on 3D Face Reconstruction from 2D Images

Ali Moeini[1(✉)] and Hossein Moeini[2]

[1] Amirkabir University of Technology, Tehran, Iran
alimoeini@aut.ac.ir, ali.moeini.ir@ieee.org
[2] Semnan University, Semnan, Iran

Abstract. In this paper, a novel feature extraction method was proposed for facial expression recognition. A 3D Facial Expression Generic Elastic Model (3D FE-GEM) was proposed to reconstruct an expression-invariant 3D model of each human face in the present database using only a single 2D frontal image with/without facial expressions. Then, the texture and depth of the face were extracted from the reconstructed model. Afterwards, the Gabor filter bank was applied to both texture and reconstructed depth of the face to extract the feature vectors from both texture and reconstructed depth images. Finally, by combining 2D and 3D feature vectors, the final feature vectors are generated and classified by the Support Vector Machine (SVM). Favorable outcomes were acquired for facial expression recognition on the available image database based on the proposed method compared to several state-of-the-arts in facial expression recognition.

1   Introduction

Facial expression recognition is one of the most difficult and challenging tasks in computer vision because of unknown changes in the expression of human faces. Facial expression recognition from static images is a more challenging problem than from dynamic images because less information for expression actions is available. However, information in a single image is sometimes enough for expression recognition, and in many applications it is also useful to recognize a single image's facial expression. Generally, facial expression recognition encompasses two main steps: feature extraction and classification [1]. The method used in feature extraction should give adequate features, otherwise it will be misclassified. Hence, there are many methods to extract the features that robustly recognize facial expression under the restriction of one 2D single training sample for each class as static methods. The common facial expression recognition approaches based on manner of feature extraction can be mostly categorized into two separate types: geometric-based and appearance-based methods [1].

Geometric features contain information about the location and shape of facial features. Geometric features are more sensitive to noise and tracking errors than appearance features. An example of these methods is the graph-based method [2-4], which utilizes several facial components to make a representation of the face and process it.

© Springer International Publishing Switzerland 2015
Q. Ji et al. (Eds.): FFER 2014, LNCS 8912, pp. 46–57, 2015.
DOI: 10.1007/978-3-319-13737-7_5

The appearance-based approaches [5, 6] utilize image filters; either on the whole face to construct global features, or several particular face-regions to construct local features, in order to extract the appearance changes in the face image. The performance of the appearance-based methods is excellent in a constrained environment but their performance degrades in environmental variation [7]. Appearance-based methods have been heavily employed in this domain with great success. Popular approaches are Gabor wavelets [8], Local Binary Patterns (LBP) operator [9, 10], Local phase quantization (LPQ) [11], and subspace learning methods, such as, Eigenfaces [12], Principal Component Analysis (PCA) [12], Linear Discriminant Analysis (LDA) [13], and etc.

Recently, Heo [14] proposed Generic Elastic Models (GEMs) as a novel impressive, fast and trustworthy 3D reconstruction technique from a single 2D image. In fact, this method planned a 3D face model that could be efficiently produced by using generic depth models that could be elastically deformed to align with facial landmarks.

In this paper, a new combined feature extraction approach was proposed for person-independent facial expression recognition. Accordingly, a 3D model was initially reconstructed from 2D frontal face images with facial expression. To reconstruct a 3D model from each human frontal face with facial expression, a Facial Expression Generic Elastic Model (FE-GEM) was proposed. The FE-GEM method for facial expression invariant 3D face reconstruction was the extension of the GEM [14] to resolve the drawback of handling facial expression in 3D face reconstruction. Then, the texture and depth images were extracted from reconstructed models. Afterwards, the Gabor filter bank was applied to both texture and reconstructed depth images for feature extraction. Finally, by combining texture and depth feature vectors, the final feature vectors are generated and classified by the Support Vector Machine (SVM). To discover the impact of adding the depth images through 3D face reconstruction, the proposed method was compared with several state-of-the-art methods. In these comparisons, first the impact of several appearance-based methods were reviewed for feature extraction from only the face texture images; then, in these methods, the effect of adding the depth images for feature extraction were investigated based on the proposed method.

This paper is organized as follows: Section 2 describes the 3D face modeling method from a single frontal face image. In section 3, the feature extraction manner of the Gabor filter bank is proposed for facial expression recognition. Experimental evaluations are given in section 4 and conclusions are presented in section 5.

2 Facial Expression Generic Elastic Model

In order to construct a 3D face model from the arbitrary frontal image with/without facial expression, a Facial Expression Generic Elastic Model (FE-GEM), which is the extended GEM [14] method, was used due to its facial expression invariant 3D face reconstruction.

In this section, facial expression depth alterations in 3D human face models are examined and the method is presented for facial expression invariant 3D reconstruction from only frontal images. By investigating and analyzing the 3D human face with facial expression by Zhao et al. [15], the conclusion was obtained that maximum depth variation of neutral models was related to happy expression models and surprised expression models. Therefore, three models were employed to be utilized in the GEM framework. Fig. 1 shows three models including surprised mean model (SMM), neutral mean model (NMM) and happy mean model (HMM), which are generated from the Bosphorus 3D database [16] by the proposed method for generating the generic model in [14].

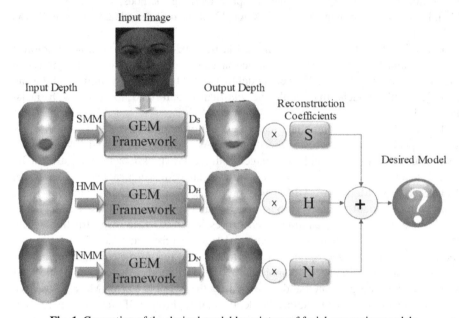

Fig. 1. Generation of the desired model by mixture of facial expression models

By employing three generic models in the GEM framework and achieving three GEM models from input images, the desired model can be generated with a mixture of these three new models according to the similarity coefficients. An illustration of the problem is shown in Fig. 1. Therefore, the desired model is achieved as:

$$D = S \times D_S + N \times D_N + H \times D_H \tag{1}$$

where D is the desired depth model, D_S is surprised output depth model of GEM (Fig. 1), D_N is neutral output depth model of GEM, D_H is happy output depth model of GEM and S, N and H are surprised, neutral and happy coefficients, respectively.

By investigating the 2D face image and corresponding depth, reconstruction coefficients were obtained by computing the distance ratio (DR) in 2D face input images as:

$$DR = \frac{d_{CR-CL}}{d_{SU-SD}} \tag{2}$$

where $d_{CR\text{-}CL}$ is the distance between cheek right landmark (CR) and cheek left landmark (CL), $d_{SU\text{-}SD}$ is the distance between stomion upper landmark (SU) and stomion down landmark (SD), as shown in Fig. 2.

The Similarity parameter (SP) is written as:

$$SP_i = DR_i - DR, i = S, N, H \tag{3}$$

where DR_i are the distance ratio in surprise mean model (i=S), neutral mean model (i=N) and happy mean model (i=H), and DR is the distance ratio in the 2D face input image.

Thus, the reconstruction coefficient was obtained as:

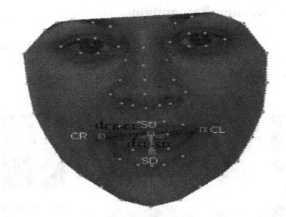

Fig. 2. 72 landmarking schemes used by CLM [21]. SU is stomion upper landmark, SD is stomion down landmark, CR is cheek right landmark, CL is cheek left landmark, dCR-CL is distance between CR and CL, dSU-SD is distance between SD and SU.

$$S = \frac{SP_S}{SP_S + SP_N + SP_H} \tag{4}$$

$$N = \frac{SP_N}{SP_S + SP_N + SP_H} \tag{5}$$

$$H = \frac{SP_H}{SP_S + SP_N + SP_H} \tag{6}$$

where S+N+H=1, S, N, H can be positive or negative.

To evaluate the reconstructed models depth error was computed per pixel as:

$$z_E = \frac{|z_{rec}(x, y) - z_{GT}(x, y)|}{z_{GT}(x, y)} \tag{7}$$

where $z_{GT}(x, y)$ denotes ground truth 3D scanned depth values and $z_{rec}(x, y)$ is depth value of reconstructed models.

In Fig. 3, outcomes of the reconstruction were exhibited for images which were rendered from the Bosphorus models in a variety of facial expressions. In the figure, three examples are shown and in each example, face image and triplet of models are given from left to right, respectively: ground truth 3D scanned model, reconstruction by GEM shape and presented reconstructed (FE-GEM) shape. Also, two depth error images were exhibited: between the ground truth 3D scanned model and GEM reconstruction model (left) and between the proposed reconstruction (FE-GEM) model and ground truth 3D scanned model (right). The values under each of the error images indicate mean error and the corresponding standard deviation (in percentage).

3   Facial Expression Recognition

In this section, the feature extraction method is proposed from 2D images by the Gabor filter bank [17] based on 3D face reconstruction for facial expression recognition. Then, the method for facial expression recognition is represented.

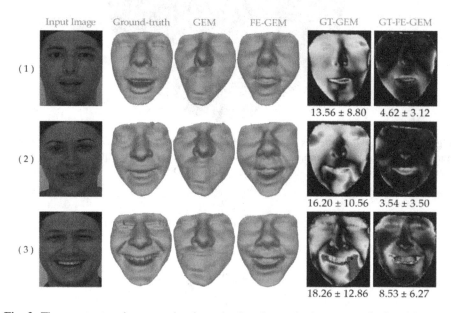

Fig. 3. Three reconstruction examples from the Bosphorus database were displayed in each example, from left to right, respectively: the frontal face image, a triplet of models (ground truth 3D scanned model, reconstruction by GEM approach and our reconstruction method (FE-GEM)), and depth error maps between the ground truth 3D scanned model and the GEM reconstruction (left) and between our reconstruction and the ground truth 3D scanned model (right). The color range goes from dim blue to dim red (corresponding to a depth error begins from 0 to 50). The values under each of the error images illustrate the means and standard deviations of these depth errors in percentages.

3.1   Feature Extraction by the Gabor Filter Bank

Visual illustration of the proposed method to extract the feature by the Gabor filter bank [17] for facial expression recognition is shown in Fig. 4. Based on the proposed method, the process can be summarized as follows:

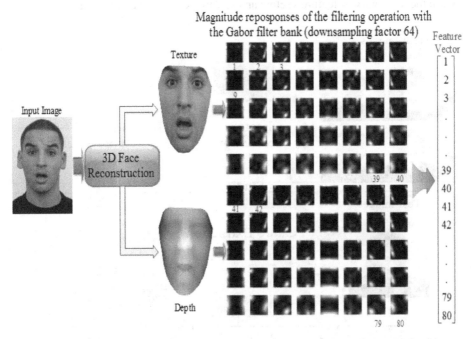

Fig. 4. Visual illustration of feature extraction by Gabor filter bank from frontal face images

1- Input: a 2D face image.
2- For each input face image, a 3D face was reconstructed and the texture and depth images were extracted from reconstructed models.
3- The feature vectors were extracted based on Fig. 4 from each of the depth and texture images by the Gabor filter bank. Finally, the feature vector was created by the entire features based on Fig. 4.
4- Output: feature vector.

To extract the Gabor feature based on Fig. 4, a Gabor filter bank with a size of 40 (5*8 with 8 directions and 5 magnitudes) was applied to each image of the pose matrix. Then, a feature vector was created from the entire 40 magnitude of 40 Gabor filter bank which was low dimensional by the downsampling method.

3.2   Facial Expression Recognition System

Visual illustration of the facial expression recognition system proposed in this paper is shown in Fig. 5. The proposed system operated in two offline and online stages. In the offline stage, feature vectors were extracted from a single frontal face image of each person in a specific facial expression based on Fig. 4. Then, a dictionary of feature vectors was generated for the 7-class (including neutral, sad, angry, fearful, disgusted, happy and surprised) training process. In the online stage, similarity, feature vectors were extracted from test images based on Fig. 4. Finally, facial expression recognition was performed by the Support Vector Machine (SVM) [18] (linear) between the dictionary of feature vectors and feature vector of the test image.

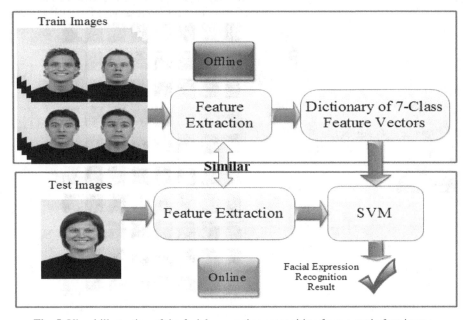

Fig. 5. Visual illustration of the facial expression recognition from a static face image

4   Experiments

In this section, person-independent facial expression recognition was performed based on the proposed method in the previous section. For this experiment, a subset of the Radboud database with seven different facial expressions was used for testing images. The Radboud faces database [19] included 20 Caucasian male adults, 19 Caucasian female adults, 18 Moroccan male adults, 6 Caucasian female children and 4 Caucasian male children and face images of each person were captured with three different gaze directions. The seven expressions include neutral, sad, angry, fearful, disgusted, happy and surprised. In this part of the work, a subset of 57 subjects were utilized which included 20 Caucasian males, 19 Caucasian females and 18 Moroccan males in seven facial expressions and three different gaze directions. Examples of the seven facial expressions and three different gaze directions in the Radboud faces database are shown in Fig. 6. Therefore, there are 171 (57*3) images from 57 people for each facial expression. Hence, the total number of images utilized in this experiment for seven facial expressions are 1197 (171*7).

To evaluate the generalization performance to novel subjects, a 10-fold cross-validation testing scheme was adopted in the present experiments for person-independent facial expression recognition. The confusion matrices of 6-class and 7-class recognition by the proposed method are shown in Tables 1 and 2, respectively.

Fig. 6. Sample of the face images utilized for the present experiments with facial expressions

Table 1. Confusion Matrix of 6-Class Facial Expression Recognition Using Proposed Method

%	happy	disgusted	fearful	surprised	angry	sad
happy	**98.9**	0.3	0.3	0	0.4	0.1
disgusted	0.3	**97.9**	1.1	0.5	0	0.2
fearful	0	0.9	**98.6**	0.5	0	0
surprised	0	0	0	**100**	0	0
angry	0	0	0	0	**98.5**	1.5
sad	0	0	0	0	0.7	**99.3**

Table 2. Confusion Matrix of 7-Class Facial Expression Recognition Using Proposed Method

%	neutral	happy	disgusted	fearful	surprised	angry	sad
neutral	**96.9**	0	0	0	0	1.8	1.3
happy	0.5	**98.6**	0.3	0.3	0	0.3	0
disgusted	0	0.3	**97.9**	1.1	0.5	0	0.2
fearful	0	0	0.9	**98.6**	0.5	0	0
surprised	0	0	0	0	**100**	0	0
angry	2.1	0	0	0	0	**96.7**	1.2
sad	1.4	0	0	0	0	0.5	**98.1**

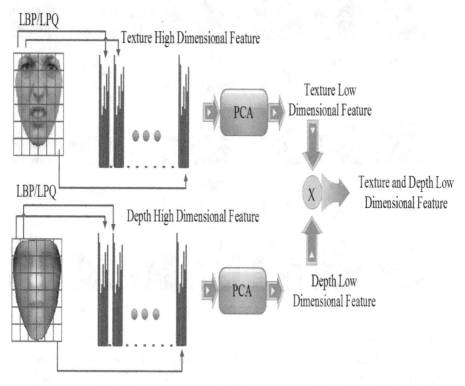

Fig. 7. Visual illustration of feature extraction by LBP/LPQ from frontal face images using Principal Component Analysis (PCA)

Moreover, to more accurately evaluate the present method for facial expression recognition from static images in the gallery, the obtained results were compared with seven feature extraction methods for test and using the SVM (linear) classifier to classify the features:

1- Local Binary Pattern (LBP) [9, 10] method. In this method, the LBP operator was applied to only the texture image for feature extraction according to that implemented in [9, 10] and based on Fig. 7.

2- LBP+FE-GEM method. In this method, the LBP operator was applied to both texture and depth images which are reconstructed by the FE-GEM method instead of applying it to texture. Then, the feature vector was created by combining the extracted features on both texture and depth images based on Fig. 7.

3- Gabor filters bank method. In this method, feature vectors were created by applying the Gabor filter bank to only the texture image and based on Fig. 4.

4- Local phase quantization (LPQ) [11] method. In this method, the LPQ operator was applied to only the texture image for feature extraction based on Fig. 7.

5- LPQ+FE-GEM method. In this method, the LPQ operator was applied to both texture and depth images instead of applying it to texture. Then, the feature vector was created by combining the extracted features both texture and depth images based on Fig. 7.

6- Downsampling [20] method of images with size 12×10. In this method, the feature vectors were created by the downsampling process on only texture images in which the length of feature vectors is 120.

7- Downsampling+FE-GEM method. In this method, the feature vectors were created by the downsampling process on both texture and depth images in which the length of feature vectors is 240.

The proposed facial expression recognition method seems to outperform the other implemented approaches. These measurement results are shown in Table 3. Table 3 shows the best recognition rates of the proposed methods, in comparison with other methods. Also, the recognition was conducted using SVM with different kernels to classify the facial expressions. Table 4 compares the performances with the SVM classifier in the mentioned method. As it is obvious from the results, performance of the present method for person-independent facial expression recognition was improved rather than methods that used only texture images to extract the features. Thus, the reconstructed depth from a single frontal image is effective in feature extraction based on the proposed method.

Table 3. Recognition Rate on the Radboud Face Database for Several Methods

Method	6-class	7-class
LBP [9, 10]	89.2	86.5
LBP+FE-GEM	**96.2**	**94.5**
Gabor [17]	84.7	83.1
Gabor+FE-GEM	**98.8**	**98.1**
LPQ [11]	87.5	84.8
LPQ+FE-GEM	**96.9**	**94.4**
Downsampling [20]	80.2	79
Downsampling+FE-GEM	**92.4**	**90.8**

Table 4. Expression Recognition Accuracy of Proposed Method Using SVM with Different Kernels on the Radboud Face Database

Method	SVM (linear)	SVM (polynomial)	SVM (RBF)
LBP [9, 10]	89.2	89.9	91
LBP+FE-GEM	**96.2**	**96.3**	**97.1**
Gabor [17]	84.7	84.4	85.2
Gabor+FE-GEM	**98.8**	**98.5**	**99**
LPQ [11]	87.5	87.5	89.6
LPQ+FE-GEM	**96.9**	**97**	**96.8**
Downsampling [20]	80.2	82.9	83.8
Downsampling+FE-GEM	**92.4**	**92.8**	**94.2**

5   Conclusion

In this paper, a new feature extraction approach was proposed for person-independent facial expression recognition from only a single 2D frontal image (static). The proposed method was tested on available image databases in order to perform person-independent facial expression recognition. Also, the obtained results showed which impact of using the reconstructed depth of face for feature extraction was more effective than several common appearance-based feature extractions. It was demonstrated that performance of the proposed method for facial expression recognition was better than similar approaches and experimental results of the proposed method were compared with classical, as well as state-of-the-art methods.

References

1. Li, S.Z., Jain, A.K., Tian, Y.L., Kanade, T., Cohn, J.F.: Facial expression analysis. In: Handbook of Face Recognition, pp. 247–275. Springer, New York (2005). doi: 10.1007/0-387-27257-7-12
2. Bourbakis, N., Kakumanu, P.: Skin-based face detection-extraction and recognition of facial expressions. In: Bunke, H., Kandel, A., Last, M. (eds.) Applied Pattern Recognition. SCI, vol. 91, pp. 3–27. Springer, Heidelberg (2008)
3. Cheddad, A., Mohamad, D., Manaf, A.A.: Exploiting voronoi diagram properties in face segmentation and feature extraction. Pattern Recognition 41(12), 3842–3859 (2008)
4. Xie, X., Lam, K.-M.: Facial expression recognition based on shape and texture. Pattern Recognition 42(5), 1003–1011 (2009)
5. Shan, C., Gong, S., McOwan, P.W.: Facial expression recognition based on local binary patterns: A comprehensive study. Image and Vision Computing 27(6), 803–816 (2009)
6. Tian, Y.L.: Evaluation of face resolution for expression analysis. In: Conference on Computer Vision and Pattern Recognition Workshop, CVPRW 2004, p. 82, June 2004
7. Pantic, M., Rothkrantz, L.J.M.: Automatic analysis of facial expressions: The state of the art. IEEE Trans. Pattern Anal. Mach. Intell. 22(12), 1424–1445 (2000)
8. Tian, Y.: Evaluation of face resolution for expression analysis. In: CVPR Workshop on Face Processing in Video (2004)

9. Shan, C., Gong, S., McOwan, P.W.: Facial expression recognition based on Local Binary Patterns: A comprehensive study. Image and Vision Computing **27**, 803–816 (2009)
10. Moore, S., Bowden, R.: Local binary patterns for multi-view facial expression recognition. Computer Vision and Image Understanding **115**, 541–558 (2011)
11. Ojansivu, V., Heikkilä, J.: Blur insensitive texture classification using local phase quantization. In: Elmoataz, A., Lezoray, O., Nouboud, F., Mammass, D. (eds.) ICISP 2008. LNCS, vol. 5099, pp. 236–243. Springer, Heidelberg (2008)
12. Turk, M., Pentland, A.: Eigenfaces for Recognition. Journal of Cognitive Neuroscience **3**(1), 71–86 (1991)
13. Etemad, K., Chellappa, R.: Discriminant analysis for recognition of human face images. Journal of Optical Society of America A **14**, 1724–1733 (1997)
14. Heo, J., Savvides, M.: 3-D generic elastic models for fast and texture preserving 2-D novel pose synthesis. IEEE Transactions on Information Forensics and Security **7**, 563–576 (2012)
15. Zhao, X., Dellandréa, E., Zou, J., Chen, L.: A unified probabilistic framework for automatic 3D facial expression analysis based on a Bayesian belief inference and statistical feature models. Image and Vis. Comp. **31**, 231–245 (2013)
16. Savran, A., Alyüz, N., Dibeklioğlu, H., Çeliktutan, O., Gökberk, B., Sankur, B., Akarun, L.: Bosphorus database for 3D face analysis. In: Schouten, B., Juul, N.C., Drygajlo, A., Tistarelli, M. (eds.) BIOID 2008. LNCS, vol. 5372, pp. 47–56. Springer, Heidelberg (2008)
17. Liu, C., Wechsler, H.: Gabor feature classifier for face recognition. In: Proceedings of the ICCV, pp. 270–275 (2001)
18. Hsu, C.-W., Chang, C.-C., Lin, C.-J.: A Practical Guide to Support Vector Classification. Tech. Rep., Taipei (2003)
19. Langner, O., Dotsch, R., Bijlstra, G., Wigboldus, D.H.J.: Presentation and validation of the Radboud faces database. Cognition & Emotion **24** (2010)
20. Wright, J., Yang, A.Y., Ganesh, A., Sastry, S.S., Ma, Y.: Robust Face Recognition via Sparse Representation. IEEE Transactions on Pattern Analysis and Machine Intelligence **31**, 210–227 (2009)
21. Saragih, J., Lucey, S., Cohn, J.: Deformable Model Fitting by Regularized Landmark Mean-Shift. International Journal of Computer Vision **91**, 200–215 (2011)

Facial Expression Recognition Using Facial Graph

Sina Mohseni[1](✉), Niloofar Zarei[2], and Ehsan Miandji[3]

[1] Faculty of Electrical Engineering, Noshirvani University of Technology, Babol, Iran
Sina.Mohseni@stu.nit.ac.ir
[2] Faculty of Electrical Engineering, Amirkabir University of Technology, Tehran, Iran
n.zarei@aut.ac.ir
[3] The Visual Computing Laboratory, Linköping University, Norrköping, Sweden
ehsan.miandji@liu.se

Abstract. Automatic analysis of human facial expression is one of the challenging problems in machine vision systems. It has many applications in human-computer interactions, social robots, deceit detection, interactive video and behavior monitoring. In this paper, we developed a new method for automatic facial expression recognition based on verifying movable facial elements and tracking nodes in sequential frames. The algorithm plots a face model graph in each frame and extracts features by measuring the ratio of the facial graph sides. Seven facial expressions, including neutral pose are being classified in this study using support vector machine and other classifiers on JAFFE databases. The approach does not rely on action units, and therefore eliminates errors which are otherwise propagated to the final result due to incorrect initial identification of action units. Experimental results show that analyzing facial movements gives accurate and efficient information in order to identify different facial expressions.

Keywords: Facial expression analysis · Facial feature points · Facial graph · Support vector machine · Adaboost classifier

1 Introduction

The use of facial expression for measuring people's emotions has dominated psychologically since 1960s [1]. The work of Mehrabian [2] has indicated that 7% of information communicated between people is transferred via linguistics (verbal part), 38% via paralanguage (tone of voice), and 55% through facial expression in human face to face communications. Therefore, a large amount of information lies in human facial expressions. The recognized facial expressions are 6 basic emotions (anger, happiness, sadness, surprise, fear, and disgust) and neutral mode which are the main facial gestures.

Until recently, the task of facial expression analysis has been a topic of research primarily associated with the field of psychology. However, automatic facial expression analysis has attracted much attention in the field of computer science. Automatic Facial Expression recognition plays a significant role in human computer interaction systems,

© Springer International Publishing Switzerland 2015
Q. Ji et al. (Eds.): FFER 2014, LNCS 8912, pp. 58–66, 2015.
DOI: 10.1007/978-3-319-13737-7_6

Robotics, machine vision, virtual reality, user profiling, broadcasting, web services, border security systems, health support appliance, monitoring of stress and fatigue [3, 4 and 5]. Recently, significant advances have been made in the area of face recognition and facial expression recognition [6, 7, 8, and 9]. However there are still many challenges remaining. For example, face recognition in uncontrolled environments and conditions is still limited by lighting, head angel and the person's identity [10].

Human faces are extremely similar, thus the extraction of facial features and selection of an appropriate classifier are the two key steps to solve the facial expression recognition problems. Two main methods of feature extraction in the current research are texture-based analysis (e.g. pixel intensity) and geometry-based analysis (e.g. muscle action detection). The most frequently used texture-based feature extraction methods are Gabor filter bank [11, 12 and 13], local binary pattern [14, 15 and 16], local phase quantization [17], Haar-like features [18]. The drawback of using texture-based methods is that they usually produce extremely large feature vectors which make the calculations both time and memory inefficient. Also, these methods are sensitive to head pose and angle and displacement. On the other hand, geometry-based methods extract information using shape and location of facial components and use this information to form feature vectors [19, 20, 21 and 22]. The problem with previous implementations of geometric methods is that they usually require accurate and reliable facial point detection and tracking, which is difficult in many real world applications.

Generally we have found all proposed methods for automatic facial expression recognition semi-automatic and dependent on landmarks. The results are less accurate for images of subjects with blond hair or black skin. Moreover, previous methods are sensitive to head angle and pose which is inevitable in a sequence of facial expression images.

In this research, our main contributions are briefly stated as follows:

1. Proposing a new fast and robust facial component segmentation method for facial objects.
2. Calculating face model graph including facial components which extracts accurate information for classifiers. Also features have strong discriminative ability as the recognition results show.

The rest of this paper is organized as follows. Section 2, introduces image pre-processing and facial point detection steps. Section 3, describes proposed facial graph and feature extraction method. Section 4, represents and explains classifiers used in this research. Section 5, illustrates experimental results and best recognition rates achieved. Finally Section 6 concludes the paper along with some suggestions for future developments.

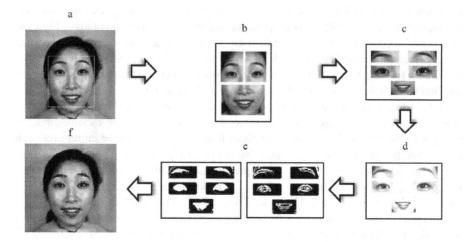

Fig. 1. a) Face detector and border remover b) Separating face in three upper-left, upper-right and lower parts c) Dividing in to 5 main components. d) Contrast enhancement e) Edge detection and segmentation. f) Boundaries detection and facial points.

2   Facial Point Detection

Methods for facial feature point detection can be classified either as texture-based methods or shape-based methods. In this study we used a shape-based method to verify 50 facial points illustrated in Fig. 1. The proposed method base on image segmentation is accurate enough to allow geometric feature expression recognition. In the following, it is assumed that images from a face-image database are being used for facial expression recognition. Relevant details on face-image database are given later in section 4. The first steps of feature extraction are face detection, partitioning, image enhancement, segmentation, and point detection, Fig. 1.

2.1   Face and Regions of Interest Detection

The first step in any facial information extraction method is face detection. To limit the processed area of the image only to required areas of the face, face detection received a lot of attention. Most of these methods put emphasis on statistical learning techniques and use appearance features, including Viola and Jones face detector [23] which is also used in this paper. The method first detects the face and divides the face region into three main parts, to remove extra borders in the picture, such as hairs, chin, etc. Fig. 1.b shows how the preprocessing algorithm divides each image into three parts: upper left, upper right and lower region. Upper parts contain eyes and eyebrows and lower part contains mouth and lips. Using grayscale histogram profile, five main facial components should be approximated in these regions. Thus, the algorithm analyzes horizontal and vertical histogram profiles on each of the three main parts. The reason for dividing facial component is to focus on local variations of the skin color, lips, chin, and etc. Fig. 2 shows an example of vertical histogram profile analysis for upper left part of face image.

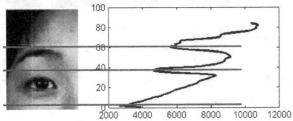

Fig. 2. Grayscale line profile of input image, vertical line profile illustrates gap between eye and eyebrow region

Using vertical and horizontal grayscale line profiles Fig. 1.c shows results after separating five main facial components.

2.2 Adaptive Contrast Enhancement

The easiest way to detect facial components is to segment skin and non-skin areas. Our proposed segmentation methods include texture and color analysis. Also, an adaptive algorithm is developed for analyzing image histogram of low contrast images, and stretching the contrast between skin and non-skin areas. Fig. 1.d plots cumulative image histogram, which sets histogram thresholds. Our adaptive method works either on dark and light skin tones. The main goal in this step is to emphasize on soft edges of eyebrows parts, dark corners of eyes and shadows around the lips.

2.3 Segmentation

Segmentation is the last step of preprocessing. It is consist of three steps, edge detection, morphological operations and boundary extraction. Because the subject's skin and hair color are unknown, edge detector methods show better results than thresholding the grayscale image. Also using edge detector methods gives accurate results while being shadows in corners of face. We use a set of morphological filtering operations to improve edge detector results and connect components together, Fig. 1.e. Finally boundaries for largest component in each ROI are used for determining facial points. Fig. 1.f shows 10 points surrounding each facial component.

Typical results of the algorithm are illustrated in Fig. 3. The point detector algorithm gives appropriate answers to changes in lighting. However in cases of head hair or facial hair existing in processed areas of the image, the point detector may fail.

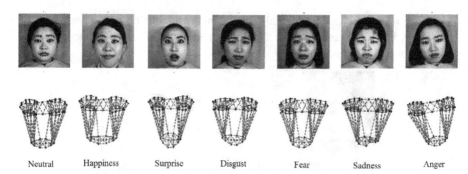

Fig. 3. Top row) six basic facial expressions and neutral face image. Bottom row) facial graph calculated for each of seven images.

3   Facial Graph

Geometric movements, such as facial point displacements and curvature changes of facial components, play an important role in distinguishing between expressions in human expression recognition systems. Therefore, both facial point displacements and facial component deformations contain valuable information.

Tracking these changes throughout a video sequence, makes it is possible to capture the changes and extract expression information. Also, drifting of the feature points is the main source of error, caused by either rigid body motion of the subject's head or deformations based on expression. For the approach proposed here, the tracking algorithm is based on a robust facial graph aligned with facial components. Feature vectors are extracted from graph sides in the form of Euclidian distance, thus vertex locations are not measured in the image. Experimental results prove that graph sides are resistant against image displacements between sequential frames and head orientation variations, but image scale variation is still a cause of error.

Fig. 4 illustrates the facial graph and the following are short descriptions of graph sides:

- v_1- v_8 = Mouth corners to eyes distance
- $v_9 - v_{24}$ = Upper and lower lips curvature
- $v_{26} - v_{31}$ = Mouth height and width
- $v_{32} - v_{39}$ = Eye region size
- $v_{40} - v_{44}$ = Inner eyebrows displacement
- $v_{45} - v_{53}$ = Eyebrow vertical displacement

Total 53 projection vectors are defined via following proportion. Equation (1) describes shape and appearance variations.

$$v_i = \frac{v_i^t}{v_i^1} \tag{1}$$

Where (t) show last and (1) is first video frame, thus v_i brings differences between natural and deformed face images for each vectors. In the current research, we assumed every neutral face of each subject as the first frame and each of seven deformed expressions as the apex video frame.

Fig. 4. Proposed Facial Graph. Feature vectors are extracted from graph sides.

4   Proposed Recognition Technique

Facial action coding system (FACS) is the most widely used method for describing facial movements. It defines 46 different action units (AUs) for non-rigid facial movements. Using AU recognition system as a mid-level can act as a bridge between low-level features and high-level semantics of facial expression. On the other hand, a particular drawback of AU based facial expression recognition is the added level of AU classification prior to carrying out any facial expression recognition. Errors at AU classification step will propagate to the expression recognition step and lead to less accuracy. Thus, we propose facial expression recognition without using AU coding system. Furthermore, in this study dynamic data is used instead of static images, we used both neutral and apex image for feature extraction. We assumed every neutral face of each subject as the first frame and each of six deformed expressions as the apex video frame. Our approach to facial expression recognition is based on three different classifiers.

Classifiers including support vector machine, naive bayes, Adaboost have been tested in the experiments. Support vector machine (SVM) performs an implicit mapping of data into a higher dimensional feature space, and then finds a linear separating hyper plane with the maximal margin to separate features in this higher dimensional space. Naive bayes (NB) classifier uses the bayes theorem to predict the class of each case, assuming that the predictive genes are independent given the category. Finally, Adaboost is a famous ensemble of classifiers. An ensemble of classifiers is a set of classifiers whose individual decisions are combined in some way to classify new examples. Adaboost algorithm has shown to be very well suited for this task because the high dimensionality of the feature space does not affect the training time. Furthermore, it works well even if few training data is provided.

5 Experimental Results

All the results are obtained using MATLAB^{TM} software. We performed subject-independent facial expression recognition using proposed facial graph. In order to verify the proposed method, we used famous JAFFE database [24]. Six main expressions (happiness, surprise, disgust, sadness, fear, Anger) and neutral are classified using a 53-dimension feature vector. JAFFE database contains 216 images of 10 Japanese female models, including six main facial expressions. Since we used 5 fold cross-validation in both classifiers, we split each class of expression by a ratio of 5/1 for training/testing. To eliminate variations among results, 20 rounds of validation are performed using generated splits, and the final result is calculated by averaging over all rounds.

Happiness and surprise with salient features such as open mouth can be recognized effortlessly. On the contrary, sadness and anger are much less distinguishable. Table 1 shows the per-class recognitions accuracy of different methods.

Table 1. Classification accuracy (%) in different classifiers with cross-validation

Expression	Surprise	Happiness	Disgust	Fear	Anger	Sadness	Neutral
SVM	89.9	92.7	83.6	80.8	86.2	76.4	99.2
Naive Bayes	75	83.3	66.5	67.5	69.8	74.6	98.8
Adaboost	86.2	82.3	84.6	75.4	85	76.5	100

As can be seen in Table 1, tuned SVM (RBF kernel) and Adaboost give about the same results for recognizing posed expressions. While Naïve bayes shows relatively lower accuracy. What is noteworthy is that ensemble classification methods achieve comparable performance to other individual classifiers, because of their weighted voting nature. As an example, here we only give the confusion matrix obtained from SVM classifier in Table 2.

Table 2. Confusion Matrix for the best Result of SVM classifier

	Surprise	Happiness	Disgust	Fear	Anger	Sadness
Surprise	24	1	2	0	0	0
Happy	1	24	1	1	0	0
Disgust	1	1	23	1	1	0
Fear	1	0	1	22	1	2
Angry	0	1	1	1	22	2
Sad	1	0	1	2	2	21

The best performance on the classification of six basic expressions and neutral was 84.28% through SVM classifier. Proposed algorithms in [6] and [16] reached to 78.1% 81.4% recognition rates which are close to recognition rate of our algorithm. However, it should be noted that, the results are not directly comparable with other papers due to different databases and experimental setups.

6   Conclusion

We presented a novel descriptor for reliable facial expression recognition. Framework is based on human vision and brain's interpretation system and works adequately on posed expressions. The facial graph or generic face model used in this research consists of 53 sides. Movable vertices allow the graph to align with facial components. Experiments were done on three different classifiers to demonstrate the efficiency of proposed method; NB, SVM and Adaboost. The best performance on the classification of six basic expressions and neutral was 84%, obtained on JAFFE database through SVM. It should be noted that, the results are not directly comparable due to different databases and experimental setups.

The key conclusions drawn from this study are:

1- Facial expressions can be analyzed automatically by extracting features from salient facial components.

2- In proposed face model graph, we estimate graph sides and different sides' ratio instead of measuring vertices displacement which causes various errors due to head orientations.

3- Features extracted from facial component movements have strong discriminative ability as the recognition results for seven universal expressions is not affected so much by the choice of classifier.

In the future we plan to test the proposed framework on other famous databases, also working with video data gives more realistic results. Furthermore, fusion of audio and visual data to understand human emotional situation is an interesting topic for future investigations.

References

1. Ekman, P., Rolls, E.T., Perrett, D.I., Ellis, H.D.: Facial expressions of emotions: an old controversy and new finding discussion. Pill Trans. Royal Soc. London Ser. B, Biol. Sci. **335**(1273), 63–69 (1992)
2. Mehrabian, A.: Nonverbal communication. Aldin, London (2007)
3. Golomb, B., Sejnowski, T.: Benefits of machine understanding of facial expression. In: NSF Report- Facial Expression Understanding, Salt Lack City, UT, pp. 55–71 (1997)
4. Pantic, M.: Face for ambient interface. In: Cai, Y., Abascal, J. (eds.) Ambient Intelligence in Everyday Life. LNCS (LNAI), vol. 3864, pp. 32–66. Springer, Heidelberg (2006)
5. Young, A.: Face and Mind. Oxford Univ. Press, Oxford (1998)
6. Wan, S., Aggarwal, J.K.: Spontaneous facial expression recognition: A robust metric learning approach. J. Pattern Recognition **47**, 1859–1868 (2014)

7. Taner Eskil, M., Benli, K.S.: Facial expression recognition based on anatomy. J. Computer Vision and Image Understanding **119**, 1–14 (2014)

8. Li, Y., Wang, S., Zhao, Y., Ji, Q.: Simultaneous Facial Feature Tracking and Facial Expression Recognition. IEEE Transactions on Image Processing **22**(7) (2013)

9. Valstar, M.F., Pantic, M.: Fully Automatic Recognition of the Temporal Phases of Facial Actions. IEEE Transactions on Systems, Man, and Cybernetics **42**(1) (2012)

10. Fasel, B., Luettin, J.: Automatic facial expression analyses: a survey. Pattern Recognition **36**, 259–275 (2003)

11. Bartlett, M.S., Littlewort, G., Frank, M.G., Lainscsek, C., Fasel, I., Movellan, J.R.: Recognizing facial expression: machine learning and application to spontaneous behavior. In: Proc. IEEE Conf. Comput. Vis. Pattern Recognit., vol. 2, pp. 568–573 (2005)

12. Bartlett, M.S., Littlewort, G.C., Frank, M.G., Lainscsek, C., Fasel, I.R., Movellan, J.R.: Automatic Recognition of Facial Actions in Spontaneous Expressions. J. Multimedia **1**(6), 22–35 (2006)

13. Gu, W., Xiang, C., Venkatesh, Y.V., Huang, D., Lin, H.: Facial expression recognition using radial encoding of local Gabor features and classifier synthesis. Pattern Recognition **45**, 80–91 (2012)

14. Zhao, G., Pietikäinen, M.: Boosted multi-resolutions patiotemporal descriptors for facial expression recognition. Pattern Recognition Letters **30**(12), 1117–1127 (2009)

15. Shan, C., Gong, S., McOwan, P.W.: Robust facial expression recognition using local binary patterns. In: Proceedings of the IEEE International Conference on Image Procession, pp. 370–373 (2005)

16. Khan, R.A., Meyer, A., Konik, H., Bouakaz, S.: Framework for reliable, real-time facial expression recognition, for low resolution images. Pattern Recognition Letters **34**, 1159–1168 (2013)

17. Ojansivu, V., Heikkilä, J.: Blur insensitive texture classification using local phase quantization. In: Elmoataz, A., Lezoray, O., Nouboud, F., Mammass, D. (eds.) ICISP 2008. LNCS, vol. 5099, pp. 236–243. Springer, Heidelberg (2008)

18. Yang, P., Liu, Q., Metaxas, D.N.: Exploring facial expressions with compositional features. In: IEEE Conference on Computer Vision and Pattern Recognition (2010)

19. Pantic, M., Rothkrantz, L.J.: Facial action recognition for facial expression analysis from static face images. Trans. Syst. Man Cyber. Part B **34**(3), 1449–1461 (2004)

20. Lucey, S., Matthews, I., Hu, Ch., Ambadar, Z.: AAM derived face representations for robust facial action recognition. In: Proceedings of the 7th International Conference on Automatic Face and Gesture Recognition (2006)

21. Zhang, Y., Ji, Q.: Active and dynamic information fusion for facial expression understanding from image sequences. IEEE Trans. Pattern Anal. Mach. Intell. **27**(5), 699–714 (2005)

22. Fang, H., Parthaláin, N.M., Aubrey, A.J., Tama, G.K.L., Borgo, R., Rosin, P.L., Grant, P.W., Marshall, D., Chen, M.: Facial expression recognition in dynamic sequences: An integrated approach. Pattern Recognition **47**, 1271–1281 (2014)

23. Viola, P., Jones, M.: Robust real-time object detection. Int. J. Comput. Vis. **57**(2), 137–154 (2004)

24. JAFFE Face Database. http://www.kasrl.org/jaffe.html

Other Applications of Facial Images

Measurement of Facial Dynamics for Soft Biometrics

Hamdi Dibeklioğlu[1], Albert Ali Salah[2(✉)], and Furkan Gürpınar[3]

[1] Pattern Recognition and Bioinformatics Group, Delft University of Technology, Delft, The Netherlands
h.dibeklioglu@tudelft.nl
[2] Department of Computer Engineering, Boğaziçi University, Istanbul, Turkey
salah@boun.edu.tr
[3] Computational Science and Engineering Program, Boğaziçi University, Istanbul, Turkey
furkan.gurpinar@boun.edu.tr

Abstract. Facial dynamics contain idiosyncratic information that can help appearance-based systems in a number of tasks. This paper summarizes our research on using facial dynamics as a soft biometric, in establishing the age and kinship similarity, as well as for assessing expression spontaneity. Our findings suggest that high-resolution and high-frequency information gathered from the face can be very informative, and result in systems that go beyond human performance in a number of domains.

Keywords: Face analysis · Facial dynamics · Age estimation · Smile classification · Kinship estimation · Affective computing · Soft biometrics

1 Introduction

Automatic analysis of the human face for biometric purposes traditionally focuses on the appearance of the face. The biometric authentication scenario requires that the facial image, acquired under controlled or non-controlled conditions, be matched to a copy acquired earlier, and stored in a gallery, along with identity information.

Recent work in facial dynamics have established that relevant personal and biometric information is contained in the movement of the face, especially during the formation of facial expressions. In this paper we summarize our recent findings on soft face biometrics based on facial dynamics, and provide the reader with a short overview of the recent literature in the analysis of facial dynamics.

Soft biometrics are the biometric properties that do not by themselves represent the identity of a person, but could potentially help in reducing the search space for identification (e.g. gender, age), or provide other identity-related information about the person, like estimated kinship [1]. In this paper, we describe three types of information that are obtained from facial dynamics, namely, estimated age, kinship relations and expression spontaneity.

Q. Ji et al. (Eds.): FFER 2014, LNCS 8912, pp. 69–84, 2015.
DOI: 10.1007/978-3-319-13737-7_7

The paper is structured as follows. Section 2 describes the basic pipeline of analysing facial dynamics, along with some recent methods in analysis of facial dynamics, and the most recent application scenarios, in which facial dynamics are observed and evaluated. Section 3 and Section 4 summarize our recent research in this area, including the UvA-NEMO Database we have collected and annotated, and applications in genuine expression recognition, age estimation, and kinship estimation. Section 5 concludes the paper.

2   Analysis of Facial Dynamics

The typical facial dynamics processing pipeline starts by detecting the face. Due to wide availability and integration with the popular OpenCV framework, the Viola & Jones face detector based on Haar wavelets has become a standard benchmark in face detection [2]. More recent variants like SURF cascades are shown to improve on the basic approach [3]. Research on face detection shows that by training with rigid templates and many training exemplars, it is possible to obtain high speed and accurate face detectors [4].

Once the face is detected, an alignment step is taken. Depending on the method of alignment, one can opt for independent detection of a number of facial landmarks, or jointly optimize a shape model that will fit the face. While the latter approach yields better results in general, it can show poor convergence characteristics in the face of occlusions and large deviations from the expected face appearance. Dibeklioğlu et al. proposed a Gabor wavelet based approach to model each facial landmark separately, using mixtures of factor analysers to project the appearance of each landmark to subspaces of different complexity [5]. This method is robust against noise and occlusions, and can accommodate different appearances of the landmark due to the flexibility of the mixture modeling. However, computing many Gabor wavelet channels and modeling each landmark distribution is computationally expensive.

Active Appearance Models [6] build parametric representations of the face appearance and shape by projecting an aligned set of face images to a low dimensional space via Principal Component Analysis. The basis vectors can be used in a linear combination to generate similar face appearance and shape exemplars. Given a sample, an iterative gradient-search based approach is used to find the best parameters. Typically, AAM is trained in a subject-specific way. Constrained Local Models [7] add to AAMs a prior to locally constrain the locations permissible for each landmark. In [8], a number of further improvements are proposed for the AAMs, and good landmarking results are achieved.

While the single landmark modeling approach proposed by Dibeklioğlu et al. produces higher accuracy in detecting the landmarks compared to these active shape and appearance model variants [5], speed of detection becomes an issue when more landmarks are detected. Jointly optimizing the landmarks by shape and appearance is still costly, especially if second order information is used. Xiaong and de la Torre introduced a supervised descent method (SDM) that improves the speed of optimization, and obtained excellent alignment results [9].

Facial dynamics are observed with a video, over a certain amount of time. Preferably, a single facial action is considered for generating the signal that will form the basis of analysis. Recent approaches perform facial registration on the first frame of the sequence, and then track the located facial points [9]. The computational cost of robust face detection in a given frame is usually higher compared to tracking a number of given points across frames. Tracking also ensures smoothness of trajectories.

Different tracking approaches are taken for this purpose in the literature. Optical flow features were used in [10], and a KLT tracker was proposed in [11]. Another early approach to facial point tracking is the piecewise Bézier volume deformation (PBVD) tracker proposed by Tao and Huang [12]. If the landmarks are accurate, this approach works very well, and we use it in our own system, described in Section 3 and Section 4. More recent approaches include particle filters [13–15], and enhanced optical flow derivatives like SIFT-flow [16].

It is also possible to analyze dynamics without the use of a tracker; by detecting the face and the landmarks in each face individually. Successful facial dynamics analysis systems like UCSD's Computer Expression Recognition Toolbox (CERT) use this approach [17]. More recently, Zafeirou et al. proposed to use a simple shape model and face detection per frame to do away with tracking for analysis of facial dynamics [18].

On a continuous stream of facial appearance, analysis of dynamics involves not only spatial, but also temporal registration, or segmentation of the input into facial events. This is the equivalent of "gesture spotting" in the domain of gesture recognition. While we do not deal with this more difficult problem here, dynamic time warping based approaches with global alignment hold great promise for this issue [19]. Given a certain facial action, like a smile, automatic segmentation of the action into its phases is another important sub-problem [20]. In Section 4, we show that this kind of segmentation provides additional useful information, as the dynamics of each phase is different, and aggregation loses discriminative information.

Once the face and its landmarks are located over the video, features are extracted from the shape, appearance, and dynamics. The possibilities are many, but for appearance, Gabor wavelet based features [15], local binary patterns (LBP) and their spatio-temporal variants [21,22] are popular.

The most prominent application of facial dynamics is facial expression recognition, where typically a classification framework like Adaboost [23], support vector machines [17] or metric learning [24] is employed. But there are also several works that target applications that may be of more interest to soft biometrics. In [25], a method is proposed to detect asymmetrical facial expressions, which inform about contempt, doubt, and defiance of a person. [26] analyses depression from face, and [27] deals with depression in a multimodal way. In [28], Yu et al. use synchrony in facial dynamics to detect deception.

3   Representing Facial Dynamics

In this section and the next, we summarize our research on soft biometric signals from facial dynamics. We first describe our facial landmarking, tracking and feature extraction approaches.

In this work, we assume that the input is a video-recorded facial action. On this video, we use the standard Viola & Jones face detector, which (for the controlled scenarios considered here) is powerful enough. Initially, 17 facial fiducial points are located in the first frame, and tracked during the rest of the video. Then, the tracked points are used to calculate displacement signals of eyebrows, eyelids, cheeks, and lip corners. The facial action we analyse is a smile. Temporal phases (onset, apex, and offset) of the smile are estimated using the mean displacement signal of the lip corners. Afterwards, dynamic features for the computed displacement signals are extracted from each phase. These features will be used for computing different biometric signals.

3.1   Landmark Detection and Tracking

Both the correct detection and accurate tracking of facial landmarks are crucial for normalizing and aligning faces, and for extracting consistent dynamic features. In the first frame of the input video, 17 facial landmarks (i.e. centers of eyebrows, eyebrow corners, eye corners, centers of upper eyelids, cheek centers, nose tip, and lip corners) are detected using a recent landmarking approach [5] (see Fig. 1(a)). This method models Gabor wavelet features of a neighborhood of the landmarks using incremental mixtures of factor analyzers and enables a shape prior to ensure the integrity of the landmark constellation. It follows a coarse-to-fine strategy; landmarks are initially detected on a coarse level and then fine-tuned for higher resolution. Then, these points are tracked by a piecewise Bézier volume deformation (PBVD) tracker [12] during the rest of the video.

Initially, the PBVD tracker warps a generic 3D mesh model of the face (see Fig. 1(b)) to fit the facial landmarks in the first frame of the image sequence.

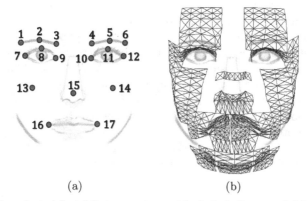

(a)   (b)

Fig. 1. (a) The selected facial feature points with their indices, and (b) the 3D mesh model

16 surface patches form the generic face model. These patches are embedded in Bézier volumes to guarantee the continuity and smoothness of the model. Points in the Bézier volume, $x(u, v, w)$ can be defined as:

$$x(u, v, w) = \sum_{i=0}^{n} \sum_{j=0}^{m} \sum_{k=0}^{l} b_{i,j,k} B_i^n(u) B_j^m(v) B_k^l(w), \tag{1}$$

where the control points denoted with $b_{i,j,k}$ and mesh variables $0 < \{u, v, w\} < 1$ control the shape of the volume. $B_i^n(u)$ denotes a Bernstein polynomial, and can be written as:

$$B_i^n(u) = \binom{n}{i} u^i (1 - u)^{n-i}. \tag{2}$$

Once the face model is fitted, the 3D motion of the head, as well as individual motions of facial landmarks can be tracked based on the movements of mesh points. 2D movements on the face (estimated by template matching between frames, at different resolutions) are modeled as a projection of the 3D movement onto the image plane. Then, the 3D movement is calculated using projective motion of several points.

3.2 Registration

Faces in each frame need to be aligned before the feature extraction step. To this end, 3D pose of the faces are estimated and normalized using the tracked 3D landmarks ℓ_i (see Fig. 1(a)). Since a plane can be constructed by three non-collinear points, three stable landmarks (eye centers and nose tip) are used to define a normalizing plane $\mathcal{P}$. Eye centers $c_1 = \frac{\ell_7 + \ell_9}{2}$ and $c_1 = \frac{\ell_{10} + \ell_{12}}{2}$ are the middle points between the inner and outer eye corners. Then, angles between the positive normal vector $\mathcal{P}$ and unit vectors on X (horizontal), Y (vertical), and Z (perpendicular) axes give the relative head pose.

Computed angles (θ_z) and (θ_y) give the exact roll and yaw angles of the face with respect to the camera, respectively. Nevertheless, the estimated pitch (θ_x) angle is a subject-dependent measure, since it depends on the constellation of the eye corners and the nose tip. If the face in the first frame is assumed as approximately frontal, then the actual pitch angles (θ'_x) can be calculated by subtracting the initial value. After estimating the pose of the head, tracked landmarks are normalized with respect to rotation, scale, and translation. Aligned points ℓ'_i can be defined as follows:

$$\ell'_i = \left[\ell_i - \frac{c_1 + c_2}{2} \right] R(-\theta'_x, -\theta_y, -\theta_z) \frac{100}{\rho(c1, c2)}, \tag{3}$$

$$R(\theta_x, \theta_y, \theta_z) = R_x(\theta_x) R_y(\theta_y) R_z(\theta_z), \tag{4}$$

and R_x, R_y, and R_z are the 3D rotation matrices for the given angles. ρ denotes the Euclidean distance between the given points. On the normalized face, the middle point between eye centers is located at the origin and the inter-ocular distance (distance between eye centers) is set to 100 pixels. Since the normalized face is approximately frontal with respect to the camera, we ignore the depth (Z) values of the normalized feature points ℓ'_i, and denote them as l_i.

3.3   Temporal Segmentation

Proposed dynamic features are extracted from videos of smiling persons. We choose to use the smile expression, since it is the most frequently performed facial expression, for showing several different meanings such as enjoyment, politeness, fear, embarrassment, etc. [29]. A smile can be defined as the upward movement of the lip corners, which corresponds to Action Unit 12 in the facial action coding system (FACS) [30]. Anatomically, the *zygomatic major* muscle contracts and raises the corners of the lips during a smile [31].

Most facial expressions are composed of three non-overlapping phases, namely: the onset, apex, and offset, respectively. Onset is the initial phase of a facial expression and it defines the duration from neutral to expressive state. Apex phase is the stable peak period (may also be very short) of the expression between onset and offset. Likewise, offset is the final phase from expressive to neutral state. Following the normalization step, we detect these three temporal phases of the smiles.

For this purpose, the amplitude signal of the smile $\mathcal{S}$ is estimated as the mean distance (Euclidean) of the lip corners to the lip center during the smile. Then, the computed amplitude signal is normalized by the length of the lip. Since the faces are normalized, center and length of the lip is calculated only once in the first frame. Let $\mathcal{S}$ be the value of the mean amplitude signal of the lip corners in the frame t. It is estimated as:

$$\mathcal{S}(t) = \frac{\rho(\frac{l_{16}^1+l_{17}^1}{2}, l_{16}^t) + \rho(\frac{l_{16}^1+l_{17}^1}{2}, l_{17}^t)}{2\rho(l_{16}^1, l_{17}^1)}, \tag{5}$$

where l_i^t denotes the 2D location of the ith point in frame t. This estimate is smoothed by a 4253H-twice method [32]. Then, the longest continuous increase in $\mathcal{S}$ is defined as the onset phase. Similarly, the offset phase is detected as the longest continuous decrease in $\mathcal{S}$. The phase between the last frame of the onset and the first frame of the offset defines the apex.

3.4   Dynamic Features

To describe the smile dynamics, we use movements of tracked landmarks and extract a set of dynamic features separately from different face regions. The (normalized) eye aperture $\mathcal{D}_{\text{eyelid}}$, and displacements of eyebrow $\mathcal{D}_{\text{eyebrow}}$, cheek $\mathcal{D}_{\text{cheek}}$ and lip corner $\mathcal{D}_{\text{lip}}$, are estimated as follows:

$$\mathcal{D}_{\text{eyelid}}(t) = \frac{\frac{l_7^t+l_9^t}{2} - l_8^t}{2\rho(l_7^t, l_9^t)} + \frac{\frac{l_{10}^t+l_{12}^t}{2} - l_{11}^t}{2\rho(l_{10}^t, l_{12}^t)}, \tag{6}$$

$$\mathcal{D}_{\text{eyebrow}}(t) = \frac{\frac{l_1^1+l_2^1+l_3^1}{3} - l_2^t}{2\rho(l_1^1, l_3^1)} + \frac{\frac{l_4^1+l_5^1+l_6^1}{3} - l_5^t}{2\rho(l_4^1, l_6^1)}, \tag{7}$$

$$\mathcal{D}_{\text{cheek}}(t) = \frac{\left|\frac{l_{13}^1+l_{14}^1}{2} - l_{13}^t\right| + \left|\frac{l_{13}^1+l_{14}^1}{2} - l_{14}^t\right|}{2\rho(l_{13}^1, l_{14}^1)}, \tag{8}$$

$$\mathcal{D}_{\text{lip}}(t) = \frac{\left|\frac{l_{16}^1+l_{17}^1}{2} - l_{16}^t\right| + \left|\frac{l_{16}^1+l_{17}^1}{2} - l_{17}^t\right|}{2\rho(l_{16}^1, l_{17}^1)}, \tag{9}$$

where l_i^t denotes the 2D location of the ith point in frame t.

For age estimation and spontaneity detection, we use the magnitude of vectorial $\mathcal{D}_{\text{eyelid}}$, $\mathcal{D}_{\text{cheek}}$, $\mathcal{D}_{\text{lip}}$ sequences as amplitude signals [33,34]. Please note that if the center of eye is above the eyelid center at time t, then $\mathcal{D}_{\text{eyelid}}(t)$ is a negative magnitude. For kinship verification, vertical (y) components of $\mathcal{D}_{\text{eyebrow}}$, $\mathcal{D}_{\text{eyelid}}$, $\mathcal{D}_{\text{cheek}}$, $\mathcal{D}_{\text{lip}}$, and horizontal (x) components of $\mathcal{D}_{\text{cheek}}$, $\mathcal{D}_{\text{lip}}$ are used as amplitude signals [35]. Extracted amplitude signals are smoothed by a 4253H-twice method [32]. Finally, amplitude signals are split into three phases as onset, apex, and offset, which have been previously defined using the smile amplitude $\mathcal{S}$. In addition to the amplitudes, speed $\mathcal{V}$ and acceleration $\mathcal{A}$ signals are extracted by computing the first and the second derivatives of the amplitudes, respectively.

In summary, description of the used features and the related facial cues with those are given in Table 1. Note that the defined features are extracted separately

Table 1. Definitions of the extracted features, and the applications (spontaneity detection, age estimation, and kinship verification) that employ those

Feature	Definition	Spontaneity	Age	Kinship
Duration:	$\left[\frac{\eta(\mathcal{D}^+)}{\omega}, \frac{\eta(\mathcal{D}^-)}{\omega}, \frac{\eta(\mathcal{D})}{\omega}\right]$	+	+	+
Duration Ratio:	$\left[\frac{\eta(\mathcal{D}^+)}{\eta(\mathcal{D})}, \frac{\eta(\mathcal{D}^-)}{\eta(\mathcal{D})}\right]$	+	+	+
Maximum Amplitude:	$\max(\mathcal{D})$	+	+	+
Mean Amplitude:	$\frac{\sum \mathcal{D}}{\eta(\mathcal{D})}$	+	+	+
Mean ($^+$, $^-$) Amplitude:	$\left[\frac{\sum \mathcal{D}^+}{\eta(\mathcal{D}^+)}, \frac{\sum |\mathcal{D}^-|}{\eta(\mathcal{D}^-)}\right]$	+	+	
STD of Amplitude:	$\text{std}(\mathcal{D})$	+	+	
Total Amplitude:	$\left[\sum \mathcal{D}^+, \sum |\mathcal{D}^-|\right]$	+	+	
Net Amplitude:	$\sum \mathcal{D}^+ - \sum |\mathcal{D}^-|$	+	+	
Amplitude Ratio:	$\left[\frac{\sum \mathcal{D}^+}{\sum \mathcal{D}^+ + \sum |\mathcal{D}^-|}, \frac{\sum |\mathcal{D}^-|}{\sum \mathcal{D}^+ + \sum |\mathcal{D}^-|}\right]$	+	+	
Maximum Speed:	$\left[\max(\mathcal{V}^+), \max(|\mathcal{V}^-|)\right]$	+	+	+
Mean Speed:	$\left[\frac{\sum \mathcal{V}^+}{\eta(\mathcal{V}^+)}, \frac{\sum |\mathcal{V}^-|}{\eta(\mathcal{V}^-)}\right]$	+	+	+
Maximum Acceleration:	$\left[\max(\mathcal{A}^+), \max(|\mathcal{A}^-|)\right]$	+	+	+
Mean Acceleration:	$\left[\frac{\sum \mathcal{A}^+}{\eta(\mathcal{A}^+)}, \frac{\sum |\mathcal{A}^-|}{\eta(\mathcal{A}^-)}\right]$	+	+	+
Net Ampl., Duration Ratio:	$\frac{(\sum \mathcal{D}^+ - \sum |\mathcal{D}^-|)\omega}{\eta(\mathcal{D})}$	+	+	
Left/Right Ampl. Difference:	$\frac{|\sum \mathcal{D}_L - \sum \mathcal{D}_R|}{\eta(\mathcal{D})}$	+		

from each phase of the smile. As a result, we obtain three feature sets for each of the amplitude signals. Each phase is further divided into increasing ($^+$) and decreasing ($^-$) segments, for each feature set. This allows a more detailed analysis of the feature dynamics.

In Table 1, signals symbolized with superindex ($^+$) and ($^-$) denote the segments of the related signal with continuous increase and continuous decrease, respectively. For example, $\mathcal{D}^+$ pools the increasing segments in $\mathcal{D}$. η defines the length (number of frames) of a given signal, and ω is the frame rate of the video. $\mathcal{D}_L$ and $\mathcal{D}_R$ define the amplitudes for the left and right sides of the face, respectively. For each face region, three feature vectors are generated by concatenating these features.

In some cases, features cannot be calculated. For example, if we extract features from the amplitude signal of the lip corners $\mathcal{D}_{\text{lip}}$ using the onset phase, then decreasing segments will be an empty set ($\eta(\mathcal{D}^-) = 0$). For such exceptions, all the features describing the related segments are set to zero.

4   Soft Biometrics from Facial Dynamics

In this section, we illustrate the use of these features we described in the previous section on three applications: age estimation, detection of expression spontaneity, and kinship verification. We first describe a novel database we have collected and annotated.

4.1   UvA-NEMO Smile Database

We have recently collected the UvA-NEMO Smile Database[1] to analyze the dynamics of spontaneous/posed enjoyment smiles. This database is composed of videos (in RGB color) recorded with a Panasonic HDC-HS700 3MOS camcorder, placed on a monitor, at approximately 1.5 meters away from the recorded subjects. Videos were recorded with a resolution of 1920 × 1080 pixels at a rate of 50 frames per second under controlled illumination conditions. Additionally, a color chart is present on the background of the videos for further illumination and color normalization (See Fig. 2).

The database has 1240 smile videos (597 spon., 643 posed) from 400 subjects (185 female, 215 male), making it the largest smile database in the literature so far. Ages of subjects vary from 8 to 76 years, and there are 149 young people (235 spon., 240 posed) and 251 adults (362 spon., 403 posed). 43 subjects do not have spontaneous smiles and 32 subjects have no posed smile samples. (See Fig. 3 for age and gender distributions).

For posed smiles, each subject was asked to pose an enjoyment smile as realistically as possible, sometimes after being shown the proper way in a sample

---

[1] This research was part of Science Live, the innovative research programme of science center NEMO that enables scientists to carry out real, publishable, peer-reviewed research using NEMO visitors as volunteers. See http://www.uva-nemo.org on how to obtain the UvA-NEMO Smile Database.

Fig. 2. Sample frames from the UvA-NEMO Smile Database: Showing (a) neutral face, (b) posed enjoyment smile, (c) spontaneous enjoyment smile

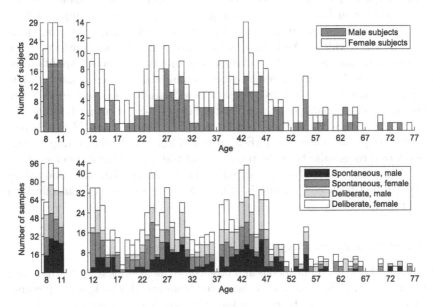

Fig. 3. Age and gender distributions for the subjects (top), and for the smiles (bottom) in the UvA-NEMO Smile Database

video. Short, funny video segments were used to elicit spontaneous enjoyment smiles. Approximately five minutes of recordings were made per subject, and genuine smiles were segmented. For each subject, a balanced number of spontaneous and posed smiles were selected and annotated by seeking consensus of two trained annotators. Segments start/end with neutral or near-neutral expressions. The mean duration of the smile samples is 3.9 seconds ($\sigma = 1.8$). Average interocular distance on the database is approximately 200 pixels (estimated by using the tracked landmarks). 50 subjects wear eyeglasses.

To analyze the role of smile dynamics in kinship verification, annotations of the kin relationships in the database were obtained from the forms filled by the

Table 2. Distribution of subject and video pairs in the dynamic kinship database

Relation	Spontaneous		Posed	
	Subject	Video	Subject	Video
S-S	7	22	9	32
B-B	7	15	6	13
S-B	12	32	10	34
M-D	16	57	20	76
M-S	12	36	14	46
F-D	9	28	9	30
F-S	12	38	19	56
All	75	228	87	287

database subjects. By selecting the spontaneous and posed enjoyment smiles of the subjects who have kin relationships, we construct a kinship database which has 95 kin relations from 152 subjects. 15 of the subjects do not have spontaneous smile videos. And there is no posed video for six subjects. Each of the remaining subjects in the database has one or two posed/spontaneous enjoyment smiles. By using different video combinations of each kin relation, 228 pairs of spontaneous and 287 pairs of posed smile videos are included in the database. These pairs consist of Sister-Sister (S-S), Brother-Brother (B-B), Sister-Brother (S-B), Mother-Daughter (M-D), Mother-Son (M-S), Father-Daughter (F-D), and Father-Son (F-S) relationships. The relationship groups will be referred to as subsets in the remainder of the paper. Numbers of subjects and video pairs in each subset are given in Table. 2. The kinship annotations were not verified with DNA analysis. This may have an insignificant effect on the annotation veracity.

4.2   Spontaneity Detection

To distinguish between spontaneous and posed enjoyment smiles [34], the dynamic features described in Section 3.4 are extracted from eyelid, cheek, and lip corner movements. To deal with feature redundancy, discriminative features are selected using Min-Redundancy Max-Relevance (mRMR) algorithm. mRMR is an incremental method for minimizing the redundancy while selecting the most relevant information as follows:

$$\max_{f_j \in F - S_{m-1}} \left[I\left(f_j, c\right) - \frac{1}{m-1} \sum_{f_i \in S_{m-1}} I\left(f_j, f_i\right) \right], \tag{10}$$

where I shows the mutual information function and c indicates the target class. F and S_{m-1} denote the feature set, and the set of $m-1$ features, respectively.

Selected features from three facial regions are individually modeled and classified by SVMs and the classifier outputs are fused by majority voting. Minimum classification error on a separate validation set is used to determine the

Table 3. Correct classification rates for smile classification

Method	Correct Classification Rate (%)
Proposed method	87.02
Cohn & Schmidt [36]	77.26
Dibeklioğlu et al. [37]	71.05
Pfister et al. [38]	73.06

most discriminative features. Similarly, to optimize the SVM configuration, different kernels (linear, polynomial, and radial basis function (RBF)) with different parameters (size of RBF kernel, degree of polynomial kernel) are tested on the validation set and the configuration with the minimum validation error is selected. The test partition of the dataset is not used for parameter optimization. A two level 10-fold cross-validation scheme is employed: Each time a test fold is separated, a 9-fold cross-validation is used to train the system, and parameters are optimized without using the test partition. There is no subject overlap between folds.

We compare our method with the state-of-the-art smile classification systems proposed in the literature [36], [37], [38] by evaluating them on the UvA-NEMO database with the same experimental protocols. Results for [38] are given by using only natural texture images. For a fair comparison, all methods are tested by using the piecewise Bézier volume tracker [12] and the tracker is initialized automatically by the method proposed in [5]. Correct classification rates are given in Table 3. Results show that the proposed method outperforms the state-of-the-art methods. The proposed method provides an accuracy of 87.02%, which is 9.76% (absolute) higher than the performance of the best performing competitor method [36]. We conclude that using automatically selected features from a large pool of informative features serves better than enabling a few carefully selected measures for this problem. Manually selected features may also show less generalization power across different (database-specific) recording conditions.

4.3   Age Estimation

To able to improve automatic age estimation, we have proposed to combine expression dynamics with appearance features [33]. Our hypothesis is that aging effects the speed with which facial expressions are formed on the face. It is well known that the elastic fibres on the face show fraying and fragmentation at advancing age [39]. By leveraging the movement features of points of interest on the face, we can improve age estimation over systems that use solely appearance-based cues. To this end, the dynamic features described in Section 3.4 are extracted from eyelid, cheek, and lip corner movements. After a feature selection procedure (using mRMR), the most informative dynamic features are combined with uniform Local Binary Patterns (LBP) on gray scale images. Since the onset of a facial expression starts with a neutral face, the first frame of the previously detected onset phase is selected to extract appearance features. LBP features are extracted from 7 × 5 non-overlapping (equally-sized) blocks on the face image.

The dimensionality of the appearance feature vectors is reduced by Principal Component Analysis (PCA) so as to retain 99.99% of the variance.

In our system, we use a two-level classification scheme for age estimation. In the first level, one-vs-all SVM classifiers are used to classify the age of a subject into seven age groups of 10 years $(8 - 17, 18 - 27, \ldots, 68 - 77)$. Then, the age of the subject is fine-tuned using an SVM regressor which is specifically trained for the related age group. For a better estimation, the regressor of each age group is trained with an age interval of ± 10 years of group boundaries. Then the results are limited with the age range (if the estimated age is less/more than the group boundaries, it is set to minimum/maximum age of the group). The resulting estimation of the age is given as an integer with 1 year resolution.

A two level 10-fold cross-validation scheme is used in our experiments. System parameters are tested on the validation set and the configuration with the minimum validation error is selected. The test partition of the dataset is not used for parameter optimization.

As shown in Table 4, using only facial dynamics is not sufficient for an accurate age estimation system. Mean Absolute Error (MAE) of using dynamic features is 11.69 (± 12.02) years, where the MAE for facial appearance is only 5.64 (± 5.90) years. Nevertheless, by combining the dynamic and appearance features, the proposed system is able to achieve the best result with an MAE of 4.81 (± 4.87), which is significantly ($p < 0.001$, Cohen's $d > 0.15$) more accurate than using dynamic and appearance features individually.

Table 4. Age estimation accuracy using dynamic, appearance, and combined features

Features	MAE (years)
Dynamics	11.69 (± 12.02)
Appearance (LBP)	5.64 (± 5.90)
Combination	4.81 (± 4.87)

4.4 Kinship Verification

Methods proposed to verify kinship normally work with images. We have proposed the first method that uses facial expression dynamics to verify kinship from videos [35]. Findings of [40] show that the appearance of spontaneous facial expressions of born-blind people and their sighted relatives are similar. However, the resemblance between facial expressions depends not only on the appearance of the expression but also on its dynamics. This is the key insight behind our approach. We verify this insight empirically, and show that dynamic features have discriminatory power for the kinship verification problem.

By combining dynamic and spatio-temporal features, we approach the problem of automatic kinship verification. Dynamic features are extracted from eyebrows, eyelid, cheek, and lip corner movements (see Section 3.4). To describe the temporal changes in the appearance of faces, we employ the Completed Local

Binary Patterns from Three Orthogonal Planes (CLBP-TOP) [38]. We extract CLBP-TOP features from the previously detected smile onsets, since the onset phase shows the change from neutral to expressive face. Before the feature extraction, faces are normalized and all smile onsets are temporally interpolated using bicubic interpolation. Then, CLBP-TOP features are extracted from the patches cropped around mouth, cheek, and eye regions. These features are concatenated to form the spatio-temporal feature vector.

In kinship verification, the system is given pairs of samples, and the task is to verify whether the pair has the kinship relation or not. For this purpose, differences between feature vectors of the corresponding subjects are calculated. These differences are fed to individual support vector machine (SVM) classifiers trained with either dynamic features or spatio-temporal features. Before classification, we employ the Min-Redundancy Max-Relevance (mRMR) algorithm [41] to select the discriminative dynamic features by eliminating feature redundancy. A separate validation set is used to determine the most discriminative dynamic features. Similarly, in order to optimize the SVM configuration, different kernels are tested on the validation set and the configuration with the minimum validation error is selected.

The proposed method is tested on the UvA-NEMO smile database for different kin relationships (such as sister-sister, brother-brother, sister-brother, mother-daughter, mother-son, father-daughter, and father-son). We train different systems using individual feature sets to compare the discriminative power of facial expression dynamics and spatio-temporal appearance. Then the outputs of these systems are fused with weighted SUM rule for assessing combined usage of dynamic and spatio-temporal features. Spontaneous smiles are used in this experiment. Correct verification rates for different features and for different state-of-the-art methods are given in Table 5.

Table 5. Kinship verification accuracy for different methods using spontaneous smiles

Method	Correct Ver. Rate (%)
Proposed: Dynamics	60.84
Proposed: Spatio-temporal	64.51
Proposed: Combined	72.89
Fang *et al.* (2010) [42]	56.91
Guo & Wang (2012) [43]	61.13
Zhou *et al.* (2012) [44]	62.16

By using features that describe facial dynamics and spatio-temporal appearance over smile expressions, we show that it is possible to improve the state of the art in this problem, and verify that it is indeed possible to recognize kinship by resemblance of facial expressions.

5 Conclusions

Existing research in soft biometrics is not entirely clear about what counts as a soft biometric, and what does not. While facial dynamics are not easily sensed at a distance, age, kinship resemblance and expression spontaneity are informative about an individual, and adhere to the earliest definitions of the field.

In this paper we have summarized our recent research on smile dynamics, and the soft biometric signals extracted from these dynamics. Our research establishes that computer analysis of high-resolution facial appearance can provide interesting insights about a person, and the features we propose are descriptive for a range of tasks. Such detailed modeling of facial dynamics empowers new approaches in soft and behavioral biometrics.

References

1. Jain, A.K., Dass, S.C., Nandakumar, K.: Soft Biometric Traits for Personal Recognition Systems. In: Zhang, D., Jain, A.K. (eds.) ICBA 2004. LNCS, vol. 3072, pp. 731–738. Springer, Heidelberg (2004)
2. Viola, P., Jones, M.: Rapid object detection using a boosted cascade of simple features. CVPR **1**, 511–518 (2001)
3. Li, J., Zhang, Y.: Learning surf cascade for fast and accurate object detection. In: CVPR, pp. 3468–3475 (2013)
4. Mathias, M., Benenson, R., Pedersoli, M., Van Gool, L.: Face Detection without Bells and Whistles. In: Fleet, D., Pajdla, T., Schiele, B., Tuytelaars, T. (eds.) ECCV 2014, Part IV. LNCS, vol. 8692, pp. 720–735. Springer, Heidelberg (2014)
5. Dibeklioğlu, H., Salah, A.A., Gevers, T.: A statistical method for 2-d facial landmarking. IEEE Trans. on Image Processing **21**, 844–858 (2012)
6. Cootes, T., Edwards, G., Taylor, C.: Active appearance models. IEEE Trans. on PAMI **23**, 681–685 (2001)
7. Cristinacce, D., Cootes, T.: Automatic feature localisation with constrained local models. Pattern Recognition **41**, 3054–3067 (2008)
8. Milborrow, S., Nicolls, F.: Locating Facial Features with an Extended Active Shape Model. In: Forsyth, D., Torr, P., Zisserman, A. (eds.) ECCV 2008, Part IV. LNCS, vol. 5305, pp. 504–513. Springer, Heidelberg (2008)
9. Xiong, X., De la Torre, F.: Supervised descent method and its applications to face alignment. In: CVPR, pp. 532–539 (2013)
10. Black, M.J., Yacoob, Y.: Tracking and recognizing rigid and non-rigid facial motions using local parametric models of image motion. In: ICCV, pp. 374–381 (1995)
11. Bourel, F., Chibelushi, C.C., Low, A.A.: Robust facial feature tracking. In: Proc. 11th British Machine Vision Conference (2000)
12. Tao, H., Huang, T.: Explanation-based facial motion tracking using a piecewise Bezier volume deformation model. CVPR **1**, 611–617 (1999)
13. Patras, I., Pantic, M.: Particle filtering with factorized likelihoods for tracking facial features. In: IEEE AFGR, pp. 97–102 (2004)
14. Pantic, M., Patras, I.: Dynamics of facial expression: recognition of facial actions and their temporal segments from face profile image sequences. IEEE Trans. on Systems, Man, and Cybernetics, Part B. Cybernetics **36**, 433–449 (2006)

15. Valstar, M.F., Pantic, M.: Fully automatic recognition of the temporal phases of facial actions. IEEE Trans. on Systems, Man, and Cybernetics, Part B. Cybernetics **42**, 28–43 (2012)
16. Yang, S., An, L., Bhanu, B., Thakoor, N.: Improving action units recognition using dense flow-based face registration in video. In: IEEE AFGR, pp. 1–8 (2013)
17. Littlewort, G., Whitehill, J., Wu, T., Fasel, I., Frank, M., Movellan, J., Bartlett, M.: The computer expression recognition toolbox (cert). In: IEEE AFGR, pp. 298–305 (2011)
18. Zafeiriou, L., Antonakos, E., Zafeiriou, S., Pantic, M.: Joint Unsupervised Face Alignment and Behaviour Analysis. In: Fleet, D., Pajdla, T., Schiele, B., Tuytelaars, T. (eds.) ECCV 2014, Part IV. LNCS, vol. 8692, pp. 167–183. Springer, Heidelberg (2014)
19. Jeni, L.A., Lőrincz, A., Szabó, Z., Cohn, J.F., Kanade, T.: Spatio-temporal Event Classification Using Time-Series Kernel Based Structured Sparsity. In: Fleet, D., Pajdla, T., Schiele, B., Tuytelaars, T. (eds.) ECCV 2014, Part IV. LNCS, vol. 8692, pp. 135–150. Springer, Heidelberg (2014)
20. Chen, S., Tian, Y., Liu, Q., Metaxas, D.N.: Segment and recognize expression phase by fusion of motion area and neutral divergence features. In: IEEE AFGR, pp. 330–335 (2011)
21. Yuce, A., Sorci, M., Thiran, J.P.: Improved local binary pattern based action unit detection using morphological and bilateral filters. In: IEEE AFGR, pp. 1–7 (2013)
22. Zhao, G., Pietikainen, M.: Dynamic texture recognition using local binary patterns with an application to facial expressions. IEEE Trans. on PAMI **29**, 915–928 (2007)
23. Zhu, Y., De la Torre, F., Cohn, J.F., Zhang, Y.J.: Dynamic cascades with bidirectional bootstrapping for action unit detection in spontaneous facial behavior. IEEE Trans. on Affective Computing **2**, 79–91 (2011)
24. Wan, S., Aggarwal, J.: Spontaneous facial expression recognition: A robust metric learning approach. Pattern Recognition **47**, 1859–1868 (2014)
25. Sénéchal, T., Turcot, J., El Kaliouby, R.: Smile or smirk? automatic detection of spontaneous asymmetric smiles to understand viewer experience. In: IEEE AFGR, pp. 1–8 (2013)
26. Girard, J.M., Cohn, J.F., Mahoor, M.H., Mavadati, S., Rosenwald, D.P.: Social risk and depression: Evidence from manual and automatic facial expression analysis. In: IEEE AFGR, pp. 1–8 (2013)
27. Kaya, H., Salah, A.A.: Eyes whisper depression: A cca based multimodal approach. ACM Multimedia (2014)
28. Yu, X., Zhang, S., Yu, Y., Dunbar, N., Jensen, M., Burgoon, J.K., Metaxas, D.N.: Automated analysis of interactional synchrony using robust facial tracking and expression recognition. In: IEEE AFGR, 1–6 (2013)
29. Ekman, P.: Telling lies. Cues to deceit in the marketplace, politics, and marriage. WW. Norton & Company, New York (1992)
30. Ekman, P., Friesen, W.: The Facial Action Coding System: A Technique For The Measurement of Facial Movement. Consulting Psychologists Press Inc., San Francisco, CA (1978)
31. Ekman, P., Friesen, W.V.: Felt, false, and miserable smiles. J. Nonverbal. Behav. **6**, 238–252 (1982)
32. Velleman, P.F.: Definition and comparison of robust nonlinear data smoothing algorithms. Journal of the American Statistical Association, 609–615 (1980)
33. Dibeklioğlu, H., Gevers, T., Salah, A.A., Valenti, R.: A smile can reveal your age: Enabling facial dynamics in age estimation. ACM Multimedia, 209–218 (2012)

34. Dibeklioğlu, H., Salah, A.A., Gevers, T.: Are You Really Smiling at Me? Spontaneous versus Posed Enjoyment Smiles. In: Fitzgibbon, A., Lazebnik, S., Perona, P., Sato, Y., Schmid, C. (eds.) ECCV 2012, Part III. LNCS, vol. 7574, pp. 525–538. Springer, Heidelberg (2012)

35. Dibeklioğlu, H., Salah, A.A., Gevers, T.: Like father, like son: Facial expression dynamics for kinship verification. In: ICCV, pp. 1497–1504 (2013)

36. Cohn, J.F., Schmidt, K.L.: The timing of facial motion in posed and spontaneous smiles. Int. J. of Wavelets, Multiresolution and Information Processing 2, 121–132 (2004)

37. Dibeklioğlu, H., Valenti, R., Salah, A.A., Gevers, T.: Eyes do not lie: Spontaneous versus posed smiles. ACM Multimedia, 703–706 (2010)

38. Pfister, T., Li, X., Zhao, G., Pietikainen, M.: Differentiating spontaneous from posed facial expressions within a generic facial expression recognition framework. In: ICCV Workshops, pp. 868–875 (2011)

39. Sanders, R.: Torsional elasticity of human skin in vivo. Pflügers Archiv European Journal of Physiology 342, 255–260 (1973)

40. Peleg, G., Katzir, G., Peleg, O., Kamara, M., Brodsky, L., Hel-Or, H., Keren, D., Nevo, E.: Hereditary family signature of facial expression. Proceedings of the National Academy of Sciences 103, 15921–15926 (2006)

41. Peng, H., Long, F., Ding, C.: Feature selection based on mutual information criteria of max-dependency, max-relevance, and min-redundancy. IEEE Trans. on PAMI 27, 1226–1238 (2005)

42. Fang, R., Tang, K.D., Snavely, N., Chen, T.: Towards computational models of kinship verification. In: IEEE ICIP, pp. 1577–1580 (2010)

43. Guo, G., Wang, X.: Kinship measurement on salient facial features. IEEE Trans. on Instrumentation and Measurement 61, 2322–2325 (2012)

44. Zhou, X., Lu, J., Hu, J., Shang, Y.: Gabor-based gradient orientation pyramid for kinship verification under uncontrolled environments. ACM Multimedia, 725–728 (2012)

Personalized Face Reference from Video: Key-Face Selection and Feature-Level Fusion

Naser Damer[✉], Timotheos Samartzidis, and Alexander Nouak

Fraunhofer Institute for Computer Graphics Research (IGD), Darmstadt, Germany
{naser.damer,timotheos.samartzidis,alexander.nouak}@igd.fraunhofer.de

Abstract. Face recognition from video in uncontrolled environments is an active research field that received a growing attention recently. This was mainly driven by the wide range of applications and the availability of large databases. This work presents an approach to create a robust and discriminant reference face model from video enrollment data. The work focuses on two issues, first is the key faces selection from video sequences. The second is the feature-level fusion of the key faces. The proposed fusion approaches focus on inducing subject specific feature weighting in the reference face model. Quality based sample weighting is also considered in the fusion process. The proposed approach is evaluated under different sittings on the YouTube Faces data-base and the performance gained by the proposed approach is shown in the form of EER values and ROC curves.

Keywords: Feature-level fusion · Face recognition from video · Multi-biometric fusion

1 Introduction

Face recognition is a very popular biometric modality which is used in a wide range of applications in the area of access control up to the unattended border control with satisfying recognition performances. Photographs, video material from cell phones, internet video and video material acquired by surveillance cameras are available as evidence material in many criminal investigations. This material can be analyzed for containing the faces of certain subjects of interest.

Some works dealing with uncontrolled face recognition used hand crafted image features such as SIFT [12] and Local Binary Patterns [16]. Higher performances were obtained by combining more than one of those methods [23].

The face recognition technology evolved from feature based approaches into appearance based holistic methodologies. Some of the well-studied techniques are the Principle Component Analysis (PCA) [1] and the Linear Discriminant analysis (LDA) [14].

In an effort to build face verification algorithms that are more robust to variations in facial appearances than traditional holistic approaches, researchers proposed the use of local appearance based face recognition. An example of

© Springer International Publishing Switzerland 2015
Q. Ji et al. (Eds.): FFER 2014, LNCS 8912, pp. 85–98, 2015.
DOI: 10.1007/978-3-319-13737-7_8

such a method is the block based Discrete Cosine Transform (DCT) that was shown to outperform similar holistic appearance based approaches [5]. Following the advances in local appearance based face recognition, Fratric and Ribaric proposed the use of Local Binary Linear Discriminant Analysis [6] that will be discussed in more details in the following section.

The availability of large and suitable databases and evaluation protocols drove the advances in the field of uncontrolled face recognition. The main database used for such purposes is the Labeled Faces in the Wild (LFW) [10]. More recently, a database with a similar structure was published with video sequences instead of images. This database, the YouTube Faces Database [22], provides the opportunity to perform video recognition from video and multiple face fusion.

The need for a highly performing and robust on-the-fly face recognition for surveillance and access control applications drove the interest in face recognition from video. The availability of the YouTube Faces data-base allowed many researchers to develop innovative solutions for this problem. Wolf et al. presented the YouTube Faces data-base with a benchmark that compares a number of the available approaches and presented the match background similarity measure [22]. Later on, Wolf and Levy presented an upgraded solution based on the SVM-minus classification [24].

In an effort to develop a pose variant face verification solution, Li et al. [11] proposed a probabilistic elastic method for face recognition. The proposed approach was applied and evaluated on face recognition from video task with satisfying results achieved. An approach using a local spatial-temporal descriptor based on structured ordinal features was presented Mendez-Vazquez et al. [15] was also aiming at improving the state of the art in video face recognition. Dealing with the same problem, Cui et al. [3] tried to develop an alignment invariant solution based on regional spatial-temporal face descriptors.

Creating a face model from multiple face captures is performed by information fusion. Multi-biometric fusion combines biometric information from multiple sources taking in consideration certain weights that affect each source influence on the fused decision. The fusion process can be done on different levels such as, data [8], feature [19], score [21], and decision levels [18]. Multi-biometric sources can be classified into two broad groups, multi-modal biometrics and uni-modal multi-biometrics. The fusion process in multi-modal biometrics usually uses performance measures for source weighting such as the equal error rate (EER) [2]. Uni-modal multi-biometrics can be a result of multiple sensors, multiple algorithms, multiple samples, or multiple captures. In most cases of uni-modal multi-biometric systems, the fusion process is carried out on the data level [9] or on the feature level [17].

This work focuses on the creation of face reference model from multiple faces detected in a video sequence (multi-captures). This solution aims at improving the performance of face recognition based on one captured face image as well as avoiding the high computational complexity of $N \times M$ comparison used to compare all faces across two sequences in video face recognition. Two challenges are dealt with in this work, the informative key-face selection and the effective face feature fusion. A video provides a big number of faces to use, a good selection for a limited number of key face images paves the way for feature fusion to produce a discriminant face reference. Key frame selection was studied in the litera-ture for general videos as well as in emotion recognition applications [4][7]. This work presents a key-faces selection approach based on inter-user variation. The final face reference is created by binary feature fusion with different approaches investigated. The development and evaluation of the presented solution uses the YouTube Faces data-base [22] and presents the achieved performances as receiver operating curves (ROC) and equal error rates (EER).

In the next Section 2 the proposed solution is discussed in details. Then in Section 3 the experiment settings and the achieved results are presented. Finally, in Section 4, a conclusion is drown.

2   Methodology

This section presents the proposed approach to create a personalized robust reference for 2D-face images. This includes feature extraction and the proposed key face selection and feature-level fusion approaches. The face video comparison process followed in this work is also discussed. Figure 1 presents an overview of the overall process.

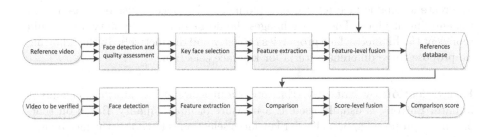

Fig. 1. Overview of the proposed face reference from video creation process and the overall face video comparison system

2.1   Feature Extraction

The features extracted from face images were based on the Local Binary Linear Discriminant Analysis (LBLDA) initially proposed for face recognition solutions by Fratric and Ribaric [6]. To explain the functionality of LBLDA algorithm, one must start by explaining the Linear Discriminant analysis (LDA) algorithm.

LDA is a machine learning method used to find a linear combination of features in order to separate one or more classes. This technique was often used as an appearance-based method in image-based biometrics, especially in face recognition [14]. The LDA algorithm deals with an image as a vector with the pixel values of the image as its elements. This algorithm transforms the images (vectors) into a space in which the between-class variance is maximized and the variance within classes is minimized.

The conventional LDA algorithm faces a computational problem when dealing with high dimensional feature vectors (i.e. number of pixels in an image) while having a relatively small number of classes as well as a low number of images per class. This was usually solved by using a dimensionality reduction technique such as PCA [1] or less conservative variations of the LDA algorithm such as the Regularized Discriminant Analysis [13].

The LBLDA algorithm aims to combine the characteristics of appearance-based and local feature extraction methods. This is achieved by initially divide the image into a set of overlapping sub regions. This division is performed using a sliding window over the image. This sliding window can be specified by size and step size to achieve different scales of sub regions and different degrees of overlap between those regions.

This work aims to deal with images taken under uncontrolled environment, as well as, being computationally efficient. Therefore, binary features were chosen to be used. Binary features are believed to provide a higher level of measurements which offers robustness to image variations [6]. Moreover, binary features give the chance to perform faster and more efficient calculations.

2.2   Key Faces Selection

To create a reliable face reference, a number of key faces must be chosen from the enrollment video. Those face images should be of a good quality and should represent the biometric face properties robustly and distinctively. In the following we propose three different criteria for key face selection.

Face Selection by Entropy. Entropy is a measure of the information content in data. Entropy is usually used as a measure of image quality. Based on that, one of the proposed approaches for key faces selection is to choose the face images with higher entropy, i.e. higher quality and information content. The entropy of a face image I is calculated here by summing up the entropy of each of the three channels of the image. The entropy of each image channel is the sum of all pixel values probability $(p(i))$ multiplied by the second log_2 of those probabilities. The probability of a pixel value $(p(i))$ is obtained by calculating a normalized histogram of the possible pixel values (here, $i = \{1, \ldots, 2^8\}$). The entropy of a 3-channel, 8-bit image can be formulated as:

$$E(I) = -\sum_{C=1}^{C=3} \sum_{i=1}^{i=2^8} p(i) \log_2 (p(i)) \tag{1}$$

The entropy values of all the faces detected in the video sequence of a subject are calculated. The faces with the highest entropy are chosen to represent the face of the subject. Figure 2a presents examples of face images with relatively high and low entropy.

Face Selection by Detection Confidence. Face detection in this work was based on a multi-scale sliding window approach. In this approach, a window moves over the search image with a certain step size and with different scales. At each position and scale the area covered by the window is classified into a face (positive) or a non-face (negative) area. This process followed the method presented by viola and Jones [20], which used a cascaded series of AdaBoost classifiers to classify each sub-image into a face or non-face based on the extracted Haar-like features. The detection decision is insensitive to small changes in scale and transition of the sliding window, and thus, multiple detections usually occur around a detected face. Those multiple detections are usually grouped to form the main face detection.

The number of detections grouped to from each final face detection is considered as the confidence of this detection being a frontal face, as the detector is trained on frontal faces. The relative frontal face detection confidence between different video frames of one subject indicates the quality of the face image (less occlusion, frontal pose, and better illumination) and thus, faces with the highest detection confidence are considered as key faces. Examples of faces with relative high detection confidence and low detection confidence are shown in Figure 2b. One can notice that the faces with high detection confidence tend to be more frontal and thus may contain more stable information.

Face Selection of Most Different Faces. One of the biggest influences on face recognition performance is the inter-variations in face appearance (of one subject) due to the changes in face expressions or the movements of the face. This face selection technique tries to find the most different faces of the subject of interest in a video sequence. This selection will be used later to minimize the effect of the face features that are not stable between those images, and thus, focus more on the stable face features. The similarity measure considered to choose the most difference faces is based on the LBLDA approach discussed in Section 2.1. The key face selection of different faces is performed as in described in the Algorithm 1.

An example of the most different faces of a subject from one video are shown in Figure 2c. Those images show the peak difference between the face expressions of a certain subject, such as open and closed mouth or eyes. To benchmark the presented face selection approaches, key faces were also selected randomly from the reference videos.

2.3 Feature-Level Fusion

Feature-level fusion aims at creating a single feature reference vector out of the feature vectors extracted from the key faces images. The fusion process is performed in order to create a more stable and robust representation of the subjects face. This is achieved by disregarding any irregularities that may occur in certain face images, and are not stable across the set of key faces.

Given a set of key face images X where $X = \{x_1, x_2, \ldots, x_N\}$ of one subject. Each image x_n can be represented as a binary vector B_n using the LBLDA

Algorithm 1. Select key faces: most different faces

Given a set of faces F of one subject detected in different frames of a video, $F = \{f_1, \ldots, f_N\}$. Select a set of key faces S that contains K faces as follows:

Initialize: select first key face randomly and add it to the list S

for $i = 1$ **to** K **do**
  select f_n from F so that it maximizes

  $\max \sum_{\forall f_k \in S} Ditance_{LBLDA}(f_k, f_n)$

  add the selected face f_n to the key faces S
end for

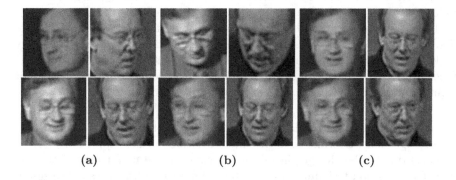

| (a) | (b) | (c) |

Fig. 2. Selected samples from the YouTube Faces data-base [22] (a) Face samples with low (top) and high (bottom) entropy. (b) Face sample with low (top) and high (bottom) detection confidence. (c) Face samples of same subject with high difference (within one video).

approach. A binary vector B_n contains K binary values that represent the face image x_n, $B_n = \{b_n^1, b_n^2, \ldots, b_n^K\}$. A binary feature b_n^k can take one of two values $\{-1, 1\}$. The task of the feature-level fusion is to create informative and discriminant reference feature vector R that represents the face of the subject in the key face images set X. The vector R is created by combining the set of binary feature vectors SB of the selected key faces, $SB = \{B_1, B_2, \ldots, B_N\}$.

Three main fusion approaches where presented and evaluated in this work. First is the *binary voting* that produces a binary reference feature vector out of a set of key faces. The second and the third discussed approaches considered the stability of each feature across the key faces. This stability is represented by the value given to the feature. This value acts like a personalized (related to the subject) weighting of each of the elements of the fused reference feature vector. The second and the third fusing approaches are referred to in the following as the *voting fusion* and *discriminant voting* Fusion.

Binary Voting. Given a set of binary vectors that corresponds to a set of key face images, binary voting combines those vectors and produces a fused reference binary vector. Any element r_k of the fused binary vector $R = \{r_1, r_2, \ldots, r_K\}$ can be given as:

$$r_k = \begin{cases} 1 & if \sum_{n=1}^{N} b_n^k >= 0 \\ -1 & if \sum_{n=1}^{N} b_n^k < 0 \end{cases} \tag{2}$$

Each of the binary elements in the resulted fused reference represent the most stable binary case of this element across the vectors extracted from the key faces.

Voting. Using this approach, the element sign in the fused reference vector is determined such as in binary voting. However, the values of the fused features are not binary and they depend on the stability of those features within the set of the subject key faces.

$$r_k = \begin{cases} \frac{\sum_{\forall n, b_n^k >= 0} b_n^k}{N} & if \sum_{n=1}^{N} b_n^k >= 0 \\ \frac{\sum_{\forall n, b_n^k < 0} b_n^k}{N} & if \sum_{n=1}^{N} b_n^k < 0 \end{cases} \tag{3}$$

This approach integrate personalized feature weighting by assigning higher value to the reference elements that are more stable across the binary feature vectors of the key faces.

Inducing weighting on the sample level as well is assumed to improve the performance by regulating the relative effect of the different key faces based on their quality. Quality measures and weighting approaches used are discussed later in Section 2.4. The voting approach with sample weighting produces the fused reference vector element r_k as follows:

$$r_k = \begin{cases} \frac{\sum_{\forall n, b_n^k >= 0} w_n * b_n^k}{N} & if \sum_{n=1}^{N} b_n^k >= 0 \\ \frac{\sum_{\forall n, b_n^k < 0} w_n * b_n^k}{N} & if \sum_{n=1}^{N} b_n^k < 0 \end{cases} \tag{4}$$

where w_n is the relative weight of the sample (key face) x_n.

Discriminant Voting. Just as in *voting*, the signs of the resulted fused reference elements are decided by the corresponding elements of the fused binary vectors. However, the effective value of the fused elements, which corresponds to their weight, are calculated differently. The fused elements here are calculated as follows:

$$r_k = \frac{\sum_{n=1}^{N} b_n^k}{N} \tag{5}$$

This approach insures lower weight for unstable features when compared to the previously discussed *voting* approach. Here, the stable and unstable feature elements are more discriminant and the difference between their values are larger.

Sample weighting can be also induced on *discriminant voting*. By introducing sample weights w_n, equation 5 can be rewritten as:

$$r_k = \frac{\sum_{n=1}^{N} w_n * b_n^k}{N} \qquad (6)$$

2.4   Weighting

Relative weights are assigned to each key face image to control its effect on the final fused reference vector. The weights are calculated based on the quality measures of the detected face images. In this work, the entropy of the image (as in Equation 1) and the face detection confidence (as described in Section 2.2) are considered as the quality measures. The weight of each image w_n is then used when fusing the feature vectors of different images such as in Equations 4 and 6.

The relative weight of an image x_n within the set of key face images X based on the entropy is calculated as:

$$w_n^e = \frac{E(x_n)}{\sum_{i=1}^{N} E(x_i)} \qquad (7)$$

When taking the detection confidence as the base quality measure, the relative weight of the image x_n is formulated as:

$$w_n^{dc} = \frac{DC(x_n)}{\sum_{i=1}^{N} DC(x_i)} \qquad (8)$$

Where $DC(x_n)$ is the detection confidence of the face in image x_n represented by the number of neighbors forming the final merged detection.

2.5   Comparison

Comparing a face image to a subject reference (result of the feature fusion) results in a similarity score that indicates the degree in which the face image belongs to the subject of interest. Given a binary vector B extracted from a face image by LBLDA and the fused reference vector R calculated as described in Section 2.3, the similarity score S can be calculated as:

$$S(R, B) = \frac{\sum_{\forall k, \text{sgn}(b_k)=\text{sgn}(r_k)} |r_k|}{K} \qquad (9)$$

where the vectors R and B are of the length K.

3   Experiment and Results

The development and evaluation of the proposed solution were performed using the recently published YouTube Faces data-base [22]. This database provides the opportunity of simulating the realistic use case scenario by having uncontrolled face images in different situations, as well as providing the ability to perform face in video recognition using multiple face fusion.

The database was splitted into ten folds to perform cross validation, each split contained 250 genuine and 250 imposter comparison pairs. In each step of cross validation, nine of the folds are used for training while the last fold is used for evaluation. The results achieved are presented as Equal Error Rates (EER) and Receiver Operating Characteristic (ROC) curves, both as average over the ten folds. The ROC is produced by calculating the False Acceptance Rate (FAR) and the False Rejection Rate (FRR) at each possible threshold value that separates genuine and imposter users.

The experiments where splitted into four parts based on the key faces selection approach used (selection by entropy, detection confidence, most different faces, and random selection). For each of the four cases, eight different approaches where used to create a face reference out of the selected key faces (ten faces in the reported experiment results).

The first of the eight approaches to create a reference is implemented to benchmark the results. This approach, noted as *No Fusion*, uses only one key face (top entropy, detection confidence, or random) and thus does not depend on feature-level fusion. The other approaches for the creation of face reference from video are based on the feature fusion techniques discussed in Section 2.3 and the sample weighting techniques presented in Section 2.4. Those approaches are binary voting, voting, entropy weighted voting, detection weighted voting, discriminant voting, entropy weighted discriminant voting, and detection weighted discriminant voting.

The results are also evaluated with an NxM comparison where all faces from both paired videos are compared to each other and a simple score-level fusion is applied to produce a final score. The results of this approach are considered as a base benchmark for the other experiments to show the positive effect of the proposed feature-level fusion, besides the clear efficiency advantage.

Each of the created references (one for each reference video) is compared to the paired video. The comparison is done with every face (frame) in the paired video sequence. The comparison with all the frames of the video resulted in a set of similarity scores for each video. Those scores are then fused by simple combination rules. The combination rules used in this experiment are maximum score (max), minimum score (min), median score ($median$), and mean score ($mean$). The combination of the scores resulted in one fused score for each video-video comparison.

Tables 1, 2, 3, and 4 presents the equal error rates achieved by the four different key faces selection approaches, the eight different reference creation approaches, and the different score fusion rules. The results are also shown for the cross video $N \times M$ comparison, where all the frames from both videos are compared to each other and then fused with simple fusion rules. It can be noticed that the results produced by references produced by feature-level fusion of key

Table 1. Face Selection by Entropy: EER values achieved

	No Fusion	Binary Voting	Voting	Discriminant Voting	Entropy Weighted Voting	Entropy Weighted Discriminant Voting	Detection Weighted Voting	Detection Weighted Discriminant Voting	NxM score fusion
max	0.3392	0.3246	0.3256	0.3159	0.32	0.3153	0.3192	0.3150	**0.309**
min	0.3764	0.3624	0.3565	0.3604	0.3608	0.3599	0.3608	**0.3519**	0.390
median	0.3355	0.3233	0.3171	0.3182	0.3221	0.3182	0.3185	**0.3153**	0.316
mean	0.3384	0.3233	0.3203	0.319	0.32	0.3203	0.3208	0.3187	**0.316**

Table 2. Face Selection by Detection Confidence: EER values achieved

	No Fusion	Binary Voting	Voting	Discriminant Voting	Entropy Weighted Voting	Entropy Weighted Discriminant Voting	Detection Weighted Voting	Detection Weighted Discriminant Voting	NxM score fusion
max	0.3355	0.3249	0.3164	0.3192	0.3225	0.3188	0.3208	0.32	**0.309**
min	0.372	0.3642	**0.3517**	0.3629	0.365	0.3619	0.3653	0.3619	0.390
median	0.3291	0.3192	**0.3112**	0.3143	0.3165	0.3148	0.3169	0.314	0.316
mean	0.3275	0.3225	**0.314**	0.3167	0.32	0.3166	0.3182	0.3159	0.316

Table 3. Face Selection of Most Different Faces: EER values achieved

	No Fusion	Binary Voting	Voting	Discriminant Voting	Entropy Weighted Voting	Entropy Weighted Discriminant Voting	Detection Weighted Voting	Detection Weighted Discriminant Voting	NxM score fusion
max	0.3434	0.3218	0.3176	0.3211	0.3236	0.3223	0.3223	0.3185	**0.309**
min	0.3769	0.3656	**0.359**	0.3616	0.3632	0.3619	0.3645	0.3691	0.390
median	0.3332	0.3174	**0.3086**	0.3148	0.3172	0.3148	0.3187	0.3174	0.316
mean	0.3363	0.3208	**0.3153**	0.3187	0.3198	0.3182	0.3208	0.3187	0.316

faces are generally better than the performance of references produced by only one face image (*No Fusion*).

In general, fusing by voting and discriminant voting scored lower EER values when compared to the binary voting, this can be explained by the personalized feature weighting induced by those fusion approaches. Detection weighted discriminant voting scored best EER values when applied on key faces selected by entropy. However, when faces are selected by detection confidence or by most different faces selection, the voting approach slightly outperforms the other weighted voting and discriminant voting approaches. It must be mentioned that recent works scored lower EER values on the same data-base [15] [3] [11], however, this work does not aim at achieving the highest performance regarding video face recognition but focuses on proving the sanity of creating face references by feature-level fusion that outperform references from a single capture and provide a more efficient solution in the case of video face recognition.

Table 4. Face Selection Randomly: EER values achieved

	No Fusion	Binary Voting	Voting	Discriminant Voting	Entropy Weighted Voting	Entropy Weighted Discriminant Voting	Detection Weighted Voting	Detection Weighted Discriminant Voting	NxM score fusion
max	**0.309**	0.3616	0.3614	0.3611	0.3606	0.3616	0.3616	0.3611	**0.309**
min	0.3857	0.3725	0.3722	0.372	0.3737	0.3722	**0.3717**	0.3725	0.390
median	0.3153	**0.3145**	0.3163	0.3156	0.3150	0.3158	0.3151	0.3161	0.316
mean	0.3207	0.3662	0.3684	0.3679	0.3681	0.3684	0.3692	0.3687	**0.316**

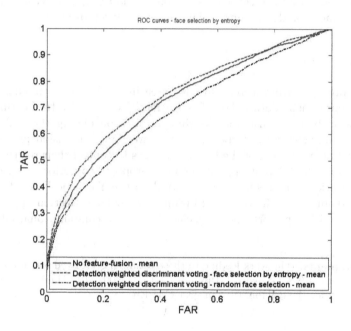

Fig. 3. Comparison between ROC curves obtained with/without feature fusion and with different key face selection approaches

Score-level fusion combination rules have obvious effect on the results when compared to considering only one face from the video sequence, *first face*. *median* and *Mean* combination rules performed relatively better than other combination rules. The best scored EER value was achieved by selecting key faces by most different faces selection, combining them on the feature-level by voting, and combining the resulting scores by the median score combination rule. Selecting key faces randomly scored comparable results when fused by median fusion rule. However the degradation in the result with respect to other key face selection approaches was clear in other score fusion methods.

It must be noticed that using Feature-level fusion to create face references increases the efficiency of video face recognition. While performing a cross video comparison requires $N \times M$ comparisons and a score fusion process of the same number of scores, video face recognition based on the proposed feature-level fusion approach requires only M comparisons and a score-level fusion process of M scores, given that N and M are the number of frames in the reference and probe videos respectively .

The plot in Figure 3 presents ROC curves produced by different experiment settings. The ROC curves show the clear advantage of feature-level fusion used to create a single reference vector from the reference video. It also indicates the performance gained by the key face selection method proposed with respect to selecting key faces randomly, under the same score-level fusion rule.

4   Conclusion

This work presents a novel approach for creating a 2D face reference model from video enrollment data. The reference model created by the feature-level fusion aims at being robust and discriminant by considering the stability of features and inducing subject specific feature weights. The fusion process also considers sample weighting of the key face images to control their relative effect on the final model. Different approaches were proposed to perform appropriate key faces selection. The results were reported on the YouTube Faces data-base with clear advantage of the proposed fusion and key-face selection approach on the face recognition performance especially from the computational efficiency prospective.

Acknowledgments. The work leading to these results has received funding from the European Community's Framework Programme (FP7/2007-2013) under grant agreement n° 261712 for the collaborative project CAPER.

References

1. Belhumeur, P.N., Hespanha, J.P., Kriegman, D.J.: Eigenfaces vs. fisherfaces: Recognition using class specific linear projection (1997)
2. Chia, C., Sherkat, N., Nolle, L.: Towards a best linear combination for multimodal biometric fusion. In: 2010 20th International Conference on Pattern Recognition (ICPR), pp. 1176–1179 (2010)
3. Cui, Z., Li, W., Xu, D., Shan, S., Chen, X.: Fusing robust face region descriptors via multiple metric learning for face recognition in the wild. In: 2013 IEEE Conference on Computer Vision and Pattern Recognition (CVPR), pp. 3554–3561, June 2013
4. Dhall, A., Asthana, A., Goecke, R., Gedeon, T.: Emotion recognition using phog and lpq features. In: 2011 IEEE International Conference on Automatic Face Gesture Recognition and Workshops (FG 2011), pp. 878–883, March 2011
5. Ekenel, H.K., Stiefelhagen, R.: Local appearance based face recognition using discrete cosine transform. In: 13th European Signal Processing Conference, EUSIPCO 2005 (2005)

6. Fratric, I., Ribaric, S.: Local Binary LDA for Face Recognition. In: Vielhauer, C., Dittmann, J., Drygajlo, A., Juul, N.C., Fairhurst, M.C. (eds.) BioID 2011. LNCS, vol. 6583, pp. 144–155. Springer, Heidelberg (2011)

7. Guan, G., Wang, Z., Lu, S., Deng, J., Feng, D.: Keypoint-based keyframe selection. IEEE Transactions on Circuits and Systems for Video Technology 23(4), 729–734 (2013)

8. Gyaourova, A., Bebis, G., Pavlidis, I.: Fusion of Infrared and Visible Images for Face Recognition. In: Pajdla, T., Matas, J.G. (eds.) ECCV 2004. LNCS, vol. 3024, pp. 456–468. Springer, Heidelberg (2004)

9. Hao, Y., Sun, Z., Tan, T.: Comparative Studies on Multispectral Palm Image Fusion for Biometrics. In: Yagi, Y., Kang, S.B., Kweon, I.S., Zha, H. (eds.) ACCV 2007, Part II. LNCS, vol. 4844, pp. 12–21. Springer, Heidelberg (2007)

10. Huang, G.B., Mattar, M., Berg, T., Learned-Miller, E.: Labeled Faces in the Wild: A Database forStudying Face Recognition in Unconstrained Environments. In: Workshop on Faces in 'Real-Life' Images: Detection, Alignment, and Recognition. Erik Learned-Miller and Andras Ferencz and Frédéric Jurie, Marseille, France (2008). http://hal.inria.fr/inria-00321923

11. Li, H., Hua, G., Lin, Z., Brandt, J., Yang, J.: Probabilistic elastic matching for pose variant face verification. In: 2013 IEEE Conference on Computer Vision and Pattern Recognition, 3499–3506 (2013)

12. Lowe, D.: Distinctive image features from scale-invariant keypoints. International Journal of Computer Vision 60(2), 91–110 (2004)

13. Lu, J., Plataniotis, K.N., Venetsanopoulos, A.N.: Regularized discriminant analysis for the small sample size problem in face recognition. Pattern Recogn. Lett. 24(16), 3079–3087 (2003), http://dx.doi.org/10.1016/S0167-8655(03)00167-3

14. Lu, J., Plataniotis, K., Venetsanopoulos, A.: Face recognition using lda-based algorithms. IEEE Transactions on Neural Networks 14(1), 195–200 (2003)

15. Mendez-Vazquez, H., Martinez-Diaz, Y., Chai, Z.: Volume structured ordinal features with background similarity measure for video face recognition. In: 2013 International Conference on Biometrics (ICB), pp. 1–6, June 2013

16. Ojala, T., Pietikäinen, M., Harwood, D.: A comparative study of texture measures with classification based on featured distributions. Pattern Recognition 29(1), 51–59 (1996). http://dx.doi.org/10.1016/0031-3203(95)00067-4

17. Pinto, N., DiCarlo, J., Cox, D.: How far can you get with a modern face recognition test set using only simple features? In: IEEE Conference on Computer Vision and Pattern Recognition, CVPR 2009, pp. 2591–2598, June 2009

18. Prabhakar, S., Jain, A.K.: Decision-level Fusion in Fingerprint Verification. In: Kittler, J., Roli, F. (eds.) MCS 2001. LNCS, vol. 2096, pp. 88–98. Springer, Heidelberg (2001)

19. Raghavendra, R., Dorizzi, B., Rao, A., Kumar, G.H.: Designing efficient fusion schemes for multimodal biometric systems using face and palmprint. Pattern Recognition 44(5), 1076–1088 (2011). http://www.sciencedirect.com/science/article/pii/S0031320310005352

20. Viola, P., Jones, M.: Rapid object detection using a boosted cascade of simple features. In: Proceedings of the 2001 IEEE Computer Society Conference on Computer Vision and Pattern Recognition, CVPR 2001, vol. 1, pp. I-511–I-518 (2001)

21. Wang, Y., Tan, T., Jain, A.: Combining face and iris biometrics for identity verification. In: Kittler, J., Nixon, M. (eds.) Audio- and Video-Based Biometric Person Authentication. Lecture Notes in Computer Science, vol. 2688, pp. 805–813. Springer, Berlin Heidelberg (2003)

22. Wolf, L., Hassner, T., Maoz, I.: Face recognition in unconstrained videos with matched background similarity. In: 2011 IEEE Conference on Computer Vision and Pattern Recognition (CVPR), pp. 529–534, June 2011

23. Wolf, Lior, Hassner, Tal, Taigman, Yaniv: Similarity Scores Based on Background Samples. In: Zha, Hongbin, Taniguchi, Rin-ichiro, Maybank, Stephen (eds.) ACCV 2009, Part II. LNCS, vol. 5995, pp. 88–97. Springer, Heidelberg (2010)

24. Wolf, L., Levy, N.: The svm-minus similarity score for video face recognition. In: Proceedings of the 2013 IEEE Conference on Computer Vision and Pattern Recognition, CVPR 2013, pp. 3523–3530. IEEE Computer Society, Washington, DC (2013). http://dx.doi.org/10.1109/CVPR.2013.452

Scalable Face Retrieval by Simple Classifiers and Voting Scheme

Yuzuko Utsumi[✉], Yuji Sakano, Keisuke Maekawa, Masakazu Iwamura, and Koichi Kise

Graduate School of Engineering, Osaka Prefecture University, 1-1 Gakuencho, Naka, Sakai, Osaka 599-8531, Japan {yuzuko,masa,kise}@cs.osakafu-u.ac.jp

Abstract. In this paper, we propose a scalable face retrieval method on large data. In order to search a particular person from videos on the Web, face recognition is one of the most effective methods. Needless to say that retrieving faces from videos are more challenging than that from a still image due to inconsistency in imaging conditions such as change of view point, lighting condition and resolution. However, dealing with them is not enough to realize the retrieval on large data. In addition, a face recognition method on the videos should be highly scalable as the number of the videos on the Web is enormous. Existing face recognition methods do not scale. In order to realize scalable face recognition, we propose a novel face recognition method. The proposed method is scalable even if the data is million-scale with high accuracy. The proposed method uses local features for face representation, and an approximate nearest neighbor (ANN) search for feature matching to reduce computational time. A voting scheme is used for recognition to compensate for low accuracy of the ANN search. We created a 5 million database and evaluated the proposed method. As results, the proposed method showed more than thousand times faster than a conventional sublinear method. Moreover, the proposed method recognized face images with a top 1000 cumulative accuracy of 100% in 139 ms recognition time (excluding preprocessing and feature extraction for the query image) per query image on the 5 million face database.

1 Introduction

Imagine that you want to find an actress from videos on the Web. It is hard to find her manually because the number of videos on the Web is enormous. Therefore, retrieving particular persons by a machine from enormous video data is demanded. Face recognition is useful for finding a particular person. In order to realize the retrieval, we need a face recognition method which is robust against inconsistency in imaging conditions such as change of view point, lighting condition and resolution. However, dealing with them is not enough to realize the retrieval on large data. In addition, scalability is required because face recognition on the video, meaning face recognition on large data, requires a lot of computational time. In this paper, we focus on the scalability.

© Springer International Publishing Switzerland 2015
Q. Ji et al. (Eds.): FFER 2014, LNCS 8912, pp. 99–108, 2015.
DOI: 10.1007/978-3-319-13737-7_9

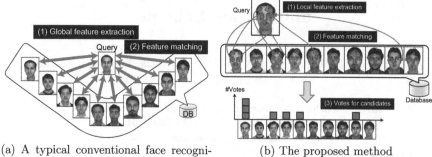

(a) A typical conventional face recognition method

(b) The proposed method

Fig. 1. Overview of face recognition processes

Scalable face recognition on large data is not easy. Most conventional methods are based on 2-class classifiers, e.g., [1,7,10,22,25,27,29,30,32]. Figure 1a shows an example of the conventional face recognition methods. When the methods recognize a face, (1) a feature is extracted from a query image and (2) the method must evaluate the query as many times as the number of persons (classes) the method can recognize. As a result, those methods take computational time in proportion to the size of data. Exceptionally, some methods take into account scalability [24,26]. Those methods can recognize a face with sublinear time to the size of data. However, the sublinear time just means less than linear time, and does not always mean scalable enough; computational times of methods in sublinear times can vary from thousands to tens of thousands.

Therefore, we propose a scalable sublinear face recognition method to retrieve face images from a large-scale data. As shown in Fig. 1b, the proposed method represents a query image as multiple local features and recognizes face images by a voting scheme with a classifier based on an approximate nearest neighbor (ANN; approximate NN) search method. Thanks to the ANN, the proposed method can reduce computational time substantially. Meanwhile, the ANN search makes a sacrifice of matching accuracy. The voting scheme compensates for low matching accuracy. We created a 5 million database for evaluating scalability of the proposed method. As results, the proposed method was thousand times faster than the conventional sublinear method [26].

The proposed method can be applied to a face sequence extracted from a video. This means that we can use multiple images for recognition. As shown in [8], face recognition using image sequence shows better recognition rate than that of using a single image. Therefore, we can execute more accurate face retrieval when the proposed method is used for video data.

2   Related Work

Face recognition is an active research area and various methods have been proposed. Conventional methods like Eigenface [25,27,29], Fisherface [1,30], Linear

Discriminant Analysis (LDA) [10, 32] and Support Vector Machine (SVM) [7, 22] are not useful on large data because their computational times for recognition increase linearly. Their weak point is that the classifiers are designed to solve 2-class distinction problems. In order to recognize a face from multiple persons, the 2-class classifiers have to be structured using one-vs-one or one-vs-all approach. The computational time of the one-vs-all approach, which is lighter than the one-vs-one approach in computational cost, increases in proportion to the number of categories in the database. Thus it is very time consuming and they are impractical on a large-scale database.

Some face recognition methods realized sublinear computational time through decreasing computational time of classifiers. Schwartz et al. [24] proposed a scalable face recognition method based on a decision tree. Shi et al. [26] proposed a rapid face recognition method, which speeds up a sparse representation method [28] by up to 150 times by using a hashing method. They succeed in decreasing computational costs, but they still have problems with scalability because they are evaluated with small size data. There is no confidence that they are scalable on large data.

In object retrieval, some scalable methods based on the Bag-of-Features (BoF) model have already proposed [3, 14, 20]. However, they are not designed for specific object recognition like face recognition but for generic object recognition. In the BoF model, local features extracted from an image are quantized by visual words, and the image is represented by a histogram of the visual words. They can realize scalable object retrieval because the BoF model can express images more compact than local features. However, quantization is known to decrease discriminative power; it is shown by Zhu et al. in the context of visual object retrieval that local feature matching without quantization outperformed the BoF model (local feature matching with quantization) [33]. Therefore, for retrieving face images we use the strategy of local feature matching without quantization, following the success of the strategy in the specific object recognition [11, 12, 17].

3   Proposed Method

The proposed method consists of face representation by multiple feature vectors per image and a voting scheme with NN classifiers using ANN search instead of NN search. The classifiers are quite fast while recognition rate is not high due to the trade-off relationship between accuracy and computational time. Thus it is hard to avoid reduction of recognition accuracy for fast classifiers. However, the voting scheme compensates for the reduction. With the voting scheme, even if the classifier performs moderate recognition accuracy, a voting result can achieve high recognition accuracy. This is because the true class tends to have more votes than others even if casting each vote is less accurate. In order to utilize the voting scheme, multiple feature vectors are required to be extracted from a query image. This is a reason to use a local feature.

Detailed procedure of the proposed method is presented. As preparation, local features extracted from reference images are stored in the database with

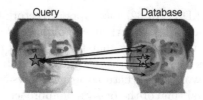

Fig. 2. Example of position constraint for feature matching. The green circle in the face image in the database (on the right side) represents the position constraint for the feature vector represented by a red star in the query face image (on the left side).

class labels (i.e., IDs of reference images). For a given query face image, the following process is carried out (the numbers correspond to those of Fig. 1b). (1) features are also extracted from the query image. (2) in each feature of a query image, K nearest features in the database are calculated by the ANN search method in the Euclidean distance. (3) votes are cast for the class labels of the retrieved K nearest features. Consequently, the class label which gets the maximum votes is chosen as the recognition result. We use a weighted voting scheme. The weight is determined based on a distance between the nearest feature to the query feature in the feature space. By letting d be the distance, the weight of the voting of the matched feature is represented as $1/d^2$.

We use geometric limitation to feature matching as shown in Fig. 2. That is, we limit the area of features in the database for matching a query feature. The feature matching method can avoid mismatching features extracted from different part of faces, though there is a chance to fail in recognizing misaligned face images as recent methods such as [2] do.

4   Experiments

4.1   Experimental Environment

For evaluation, we created a 5 million face database, which consisted of face images downloaded from the Web, Flickr[1], and public face databases: AR Face Database [16], the Extended Yale B Face Database [5], CAS-PEAL [4], FERET [21], The AT&T The Database of Faces[2], Georgia Tech Face Database [19], Surveillance Cameras Face Database [6] and Indian Face Database[3]. The samples of the data from the Web are shown in Fig. 3. We used some keywords and dates to search, and downloaded the images. After downloading the images, we got rid of duplicate image files. Therefore, the images from the Web may contain multiple images of one person. The face images were cropped by using a face detector [18] and face direction of the cropped images was normalized by using the method proposed in [13,31], which extracted 14 facial feature points on eyes, nose and so on.

---

[1] Flickr, https://www.flickr.com

[2] AT&T The Database of Faces, http://www.cl.cam.ac.uk/research/dtg/attarchive/facedatabase.html

[3] The indian face database,
http://vis-www.cs.umass.edu/~vidit/IndianFaceDatabase/

Fig. 3. Samples of face images downloaded from the Web

Based on these facial feature points, we extracted a face region from a face image and normalized face direction. Normalized images were 8 bit gray-scale and the dimensions were 512×512 pixels.

We used the AR Face Database [16] and the Extended Yale Face Database B [5] as test data. The AR Face Database consists of over 4,000 images from 136 individuals. We put the set 1 (Neutral) to the database. We excluded two images of the set 1 from the database because they failed to be normalized. We put the sets 2-7 (Smile, Anger, Scream, Left Side Light on, Right Side Light on, and All Side Light on) to test sets (query images). The number of queries was 792. The Extended Yale Face Database B consisted of 16,128 images from 28 individuals. We put 27 images from 27 individuals whose facial pose was frontal and light source direction with respect to the camera axis was at 0 degrees azimuth and 0 degrees elevation to the database. We also excluded one image from the database because the detection or normalization failed. We used the remaining images, where the detection and normalization succeeded, as queries. Images of the test set were also cropped and normalized by the same method as the database. The number of queries was 847. In the following results, computational time excludes the time for preprocessing and feature extraction for the query image. We employed a computer with AMD Opteron 2.2GHz CPU and 256GB RAM. The average number of feature vectors extracted from an image was about 200. We used the state-of-the-art ANN search method that is empirically shown to have the computational time less than proportional (sublinear) to the data size [23].

4.2   Experimental Results

In order to compare the recognition accuracy and recognition speed, we evaluated the proposed method and a sublinear method proposed in [26]. In the proposed method, we used PCA-SIFT [9], SIFT [15], the Gabor wavelet feature (real part, imaginary part and magnitude), and the Local Binary Patterns as local features. The dimensionality of PCA-SIFT, SIFT, the Gabor wavelet feature, and the LBP were 36, 128, 40, and 59, respectively. We changed parameters of the K-NN method and the ANN method for evaluation. In the conventional method, we used 256×256 and 128×128 images as feature. We also changed the parameters of the conventional method for evaluation. We changed the number of images in a database from 10,000 up to 100,000 and evaluated the scalability of the proposed method and the conventional method. The database we used for

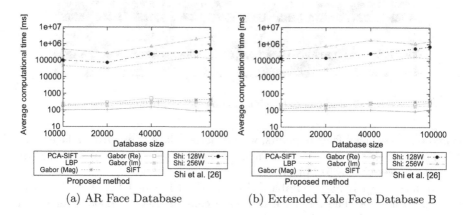

(a) AR Face Database   (b) Extended Yale Face Database B

Fig. 4. Relationship between the size of the database and computational time

the evaluation is a part of the 5 million database we made and contained AR face database and Extended Yale Face Database B.

The graphs in Figs. 4 and 5 plotted the relationship between the size of the database and computational time, and the relationship between the size of the database and top 200 cumulative recognition rate, respectively. In the graphs, PCA-SIFT, SIFT, Gabor (Mag0, Gabor (Re), Gabor (Im) and LBP show the results of the proposed method with PCA-SIFT, SIFT, magnitude, real part and imaginary part of Gabor wavelet features, and the Local Binary Patterns, and Shi:128 and Shi:256 show the results of the conventional method with 128×128 pixels and 256×256 pixels images. From Fig. 4, the proposed method with the PCA-SIFT features was faster than the one with other features. both on AR face database and Extended Yale B database. The proposed method with the PCA-SIFT features was more than thousand times faster than the sublinear method [26]. Moreover, the proposed method did not change computational time when the database size became large. This means that the proposed method realized fast and scalable face recognition. From Fig. 5, the proposed method showed the best recognition rate. This means that the voting scheme compensated for the low matching accuracy, and the proposed method achieved fast and accurate face recognition.

We used the 5 million face database to evaluate the recognition rates and computational time. We used queries from AR Face Database and top 1000 cumulative recognition for an indicator of recognition accuracy. Table 1 shows the recognition rates and computational time in each image set. We achieved 100% recognition rate with 139 ms processing time when the set 5 was used as a test set. The processing time of exhaustive search[4] was 7,685 seconds with 100 % recognition rate and thus the processing time of the proposed method was

---

[4] The exhaustive k-NN search method we employed had a mechanism to quit distance calculation when it comes out that a feature vector does not have smaller distance than the tentative k-th nearest neighbor.

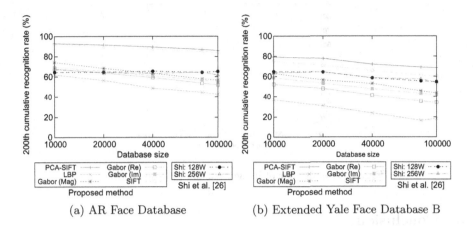

(a) AR Face Database   (b) Extended Yale Face Database B

Fig. 5. Relationship between the size of the database and recognition rates. Recognition rate is a top 200 cumulative recognition rate.

Table 1. Recognition rates and computational times on the 5 million face database

Test Sets	2	3	4	5	6	7
Recognition Rate [%]	98.5	99.2	42.4	100	97.7	39.4
Time [ms]		156	85.9	176	139	128	257

55,286 times faster than that of exhaustive search. When the Set 4 (Scream) and 7 (All Side Light on) were used for test sets, the recognition rate was lower than other test sets. However, we think that the proposed method is used for video face recognition, the weak point of the proposed method is not serious because we can choose the best facial images from a video sequence or simply accumulate features or result in each image.

In order to evaluate the scalability of the proposed method, we calculated the average computational time at different numbers of images in the database: 200 thousand, 500 thousand, 1 million, 3 million and 5 million. We used the Set 5 for the test set. We adopted the shortest computational time in the condition that the recognition rate was higher than 98%. Fig. 6 shows the experimental results. From this results, the processing time increased with increasing the number of images in the database monotonically. However, the gradient from 3 million images to 5 million images was gentler than that from 500 thousand images to 3 million images. Increase of processing time of the proposed method was obviously less than proportional to the number of images in the database. Thus, it is indicated that the proposed method has the scalability for a large database.

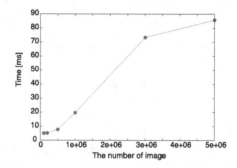

Fig. 6. The number of images vs. computational time.

5   Conclusion

In this paper, we proposed a scalable face recognition method by using an ANN search method and a voting scheme to achieve fast retrieval on large data in order to find a particular person from videos on the Web. Because of the ANN search method, the proposed method is more scalable than the conventional sublinear method. The ANN search method is fast, while its matching accuracy is low. However, thanks to the voting scheme, the proposed method showed the better recognition accuracy than the conventional sublinear methods. From the experimental results, the proposed method recognized face images with an accuracy of 100% in 139 ms recognition time (excluding preprocessing and feature extraction for the query image) per query image on the 5 million face database when images with an illumination change from left side were used for the query set. The results showed that the proposed method can be applied to video because the proposed method is enough scalable and accurate.

In future work, we evaluate the proposed method with face images cropped from videos on the Web. We can get a face image sequence from a video and use for recognition. If we can use a face image sequence efficiently, we can get better recognition results than the current experimental results.

Acknowledge

This work was supported by "R&D Program for Implementation of Anti-Crime and Anti-Terrorism Technologies for a Safe and Secure Society," Funds for integrated promotion of social system reform and research and development of the MEXT, the Japanese Government.

References

1. Belhumber, P.N., Hespanha, J.P., Kriegman, D.J.: Eigenfaces vs. fisherfaces: Recognition using class specific linear projection. IEEE Transaction on Pattern Analysis and Machine Intelligence 19(7), 711–720 (1997)

2. Chen, D., Cao, X., Wen, F., Sun, J.: Blessing of dimensionality: High-dimensional feature and its efficient compression for face verification. In: Proc. 2013 IEEE Conference on Computer Vision and Pattern Recognition (2013)
3. Csurka, G., Dance, C.R., Fan, L., Willamowski, J., Bray, C.: Visual categorization with bags of keypoints. In: Workshop on Statistical Learning in Computer Vision, ECCV, pp. 1–22 (2004)
4. Gao, W., Cao, B., Shan, S., Zhou, D., Zhang, X., Zhao, D., Al, S.: The CAS-PEAL large-scale Chinese face database and evaluation protocols. Joint Research & Development Laboratory, Technical report (2004)
5. Georghiades, A.S., Belhumeur, P.N., Kriegman, D.J.: From few to many: Illumination cone models for face recognition under variable lightning and pose. IEEE Transaction on Pattern Analysis and Machine Intelligence 23(6), 643–660 (2001)
6. Grgic, M., Delac, K., Grgic, S.: Scface - surveillance cameras face database. In: Multiedia Tools and Applications, pp. 1–17 (2009)
7. Heisele, B., Ho, P., Poggio, T.: Face recognition with support vector machines: Global versus component-based approach. In: Proceedings on Eighth IEEE International Conference on Computer Vision, Vancouver, Canada, vol. 2, pp. 688–694 (2001)
8. Iwamura, M., Kunze, K., Kato, Y., Utsumi, Y., Kise, K.: Haven't we met before? – a realistic memory assistance system to remind you of the person in front of you. In: Proc. 5th Augmented Human (AH 2014), March 2014
9. Ke, Y., Sukthankar, R.: PCA-SIFT: A more distinctive representation for local image descriptors. In: Proceedings of IEEE Computer Society Conference on Computer Vision and Pattern Recognition, pp. 506–513 (2004)
10. Kim, T., Stenger, B., Kittler, J., Cipolla, R.: Incremental linear discriminant analysis using sufficient spanning sets and its applications. International Journal of Computer Vision 91, 216–232 (2010)
11. Kise, K., Noguchi, K., Iwamura, M.: Memory efficient recognition of specific objects with local features. In: Proceedings of the 19th International Conference of Pattern Recognition (2005)
12. Kise, K., Noguchi, K., Iwamura, M.: Robust and efficient recognition of low-quality images by cascaded recognizers with massive local features. In: Proceedings of the 1st International Workshop on Emergent Issues in Large Amount of Visual Data (WS-LAVD 2009), pp. 2125–2132 (2009)
13. Kozakaya, T., Yamaguchi, O.: Face recognition by projection-based 3D normalization and shading subspace orthogonalization. In: FGR 2006, pp. 163–168 (2006)
14. Lazebnik, S., Schmid, C., Ponce, J.: Beyond bags of features: Spatial pyramid matching for recognizing natural scene categories. In: Proceedings of IEEE Conference on Computer Vision and Pattern Recognition, pp. 2169–2178 (2006)
15. Lowe, D.G.: Distinctive image features from scale-invariant keypoints. International Journal of Computer Vision. 60, 91–110 (2004)
16. Martínez, A., Benavente, R.: The AR face database. Technical Report 24, Computer Vision Center, Barcelona (1998). http://www2.ece.ohio-state.edu/aleix/ARdatabase.html
17. Mikolajczyk, K., Schmid, C.: A performance evaluation of local descriptors. IEEE Transaction on Pattern Analysis and Machine Intelligence 27(10), 1615–1630 (2005)
18. Mita, T., kaneko, T., Stenger, B., Hori, O.: Discriminative feature co-occurrence selection for object detection. IEEE Transaction on Pattern Analysis and Machine Intelligence 30(7), 1257–1269 (2008)

19. Nefian, A.V., Khosravi, M., III, M.H.H.: Real-time human face detection from uncontrolled environments. In: SPIE Visual Communications on Image Processing (1997)

20. Nowak, E., Jurie, F., Triggs, B.: Sampling Strategies for Bag-of-Features Image Classification. In: Leonardis, A., Bischof, H., Pinz, A. (eds.) ECCV 2006. LNCS, vol. 3954, pp. 490–503. Springer, Heidelberg (2006)

21. Phillips, J., Moon, H., Rizvi, S.A., Rauss, P.J.: The feret evaluation methodology for face-recognition algorithms. IEEE Trasaction on Pattern Analysis and Machine Intelligence 22(10), 1090–1104 (2000)

22. Phillips, P.J.: Support vector machines applied to face recognition. Advances in Neural Information Processing Systems 11, 803–809 (1998)

23. Sato, T., Iwamura, M., Kise, K.: Fast and memory efficient approximate nearest neighbor search with distance estimation based on space indexing. Prmu 2012–142, IEICE Technical Report (February 2013)

24. Schwartz, W.R., Guo, H., Davis, L.S.: A Robust and Scalable Approach to Face Identification. In: Daniilidis, K., Maragos, P., Paragios, N. (eds.) ECCV 2010, Part VI. LNCS, vol. 6316, pp. 476–489. Springer, Heidelberg (2010)

25. Sharma, A., Dubey, A., Tripathi, P., Kumar, V.: Pose invariant virtual classifiers from single training image using novel hybrid-eigenfaces. Neurocomputing 73, 1868–1880 (2010)

26. Shi, Q., Li, H., Shen, C.: Rapid face recognition using hashing. In: Proceedings of 2010 IEEE Conference on Computer Vision and Pattern Recognition, pp. 2753–2760 (2010)

27. Turk, M., Pentland, A.: Eigenface for recognition. Journal of Cognitive Neuroscience 3(1), 71–86 (1991)

28. Wright, J., Yang, A.Y., Ganesh, A., Sastry, S.S., Ma, Y.: Robust face recognition via sparse representation. IEEE Transaction on Pattern Analysis and Machine Intelligence 31(2), 210–227 (2009)

29. Yang, J., Ahang, D., Frangi, A.F., yu Yang, J.: Two-dimensional pca: a new approach to appearance-based face representation and recognition. IEEE Transaction on Pattern Analysis and Machine Intelligence 26(1), 131–137 (2004)

30. Yang, M.H.: Kernel eigenfaces vs. kernel fisherfaces: Face recognition using kernel methods. In: Proceedings of the Fifth IEEE International Conference on Automatic Face and Gesture Recognition, pp. 215–220. Washington, DC, May 2002

31. Yuasa, M., Kozakaya, T., Yamaguchi, O.: An efficient 3D geometrical consistency criterion for detection of a set of facial feature points. IEICE - Trans. Inf. Syst. E91-D, 1871–1877 (2008)

32. Zhao, W., Chellappa, R., Krishnaswamy, A.: Discriminant analysis of principal components for face recognition. In: Proceedings on IEEE International Conference on Face and Gesture Recognition (FG1998), pp. 14–16. Nara, Japan, April 1998

33. Zhu, C.Z., Zhou, X., Satoh, S.: Bag-of-words against nearest-neighbor search for visual object retrieval. In: Proceedings of 2013 2nd IAPR Asian Conference on Pattern Recognition, pp. 626–630 (2013)

Positive/Negative Emotion Detection from RGB-D Upper Body Images

Lahoucine Ballihi[1], Adel Lablack[2], Boulbaba Ben Amor[1,2]([✉]),
Ioan Marius Bilasco[2], and Mohamed Daoudi[1,2]

[1] TELECOM Lille, Institut Mines-Télécom, Villeneuve d'Ascq, France
lahoucine.ballihi@telecom-lille.fr
[2] Laboratoire d'Informatique Fondamentale de Lille (UMR 8022), Université Lille 1,
Villeneuve d'Ascq, France
{adel.lablack,boulbaba.benamor,marius.bilasco,mohamed.daoudi}@lifl.fr

Abstract. The ability to identify users'mental states represents a valuable asset for improving human-computer interaction. Considering that spontaneous emotions are conveyed mostly through facial expressions and the upper Body movements, we propose to use these modalities together for the purpose of negative/positive emotion classification. A method that allows the recognition of mental states from videos is proposed. Based on a dataset composed with RGB-D movies a set of indictors of positive and negative is extracted from 2D (RGB) information. In addition, a geometric framework to model the depth flows and capture human body dynamics from depth data is proposed. Due to temporal changes in pixel and depth intensity which characterize spontaneous emotions dataset, the depth features are used to define the relation between changes in upper body movements and the affect. We describe a space of depth and texture information to detect the mood of people using upper body postures and their evolution across time. The experimentation has been performed on Cam3D dataset and has showed promising results.

Keywords: Emotional state · Feature extraction · Grassmann manifold · Depth features

1 Introduction

Several vision-based systems for automatic recognition of acted emotion have been proposed in the literature. Moreover, there is a move away from the automatic inference of the basic emotions proposed by Ekman [9] towards the inference of complex mental states such as attitudes, cognitive states, and intentions. The real world is dominated by neutral expressions [2] and complex mental states, with expressions of confusion, happiness, thinking, surprise, concentration, anger, etc. [19]. There is also a move towards analyzing spontaneous expressions rather than posed ones, as there is evidence of differences between them [6]. However most of these systems are evaluated only on datasets that are captured in controlled conditions.

© Springer International Publishing Switzerland 2015
Q. Ji et al. (Eds.): FFER 2014, LNCS 8912, pp. 109–120, 2015.
DOI: 10.1007/978-3-319-13737-7_10

The goal of this paper is to propose an approach to detect positive and negative emotions on spontaneous video streams. Positive emotions are expressed in response to situations where the user enjoys its experience, where negative emotions are commonly expressed in response to situations that the person finds to be irritating, frustrating, or unpleasant. Assuming that expressive body movements and pose is responsible for independent, denotative information which can be mapped to the emotion space, we propose a 2D model which extracts metrics to detect positive/negative emotions that are highly correlated with the facial expressions anger and happy. A 3D model of features is also extracted from depth map video sequences and projected onto a Grassmann Manifold [8]. The 3-D feature set is converted into a feature vector to construct the Grassmann Manifold.

2   Related Work

The majority of approaches so far have made use of 2D image sequences, though a few works have started to use 3D facial geometry data. In addition research has been conducted into analysis of upper body expressions from 3D static data. In this section we discuss previous 2D dynamic facial expression analysis, and then go on to look at the 3D static and dynamic work that has been completed in this area, focusing mainly on the feature extraction stage as this provides the main differences in the analysis of expressions in 3D versus 2D images and upper body sequences.

Many studies have used classifier margins and posterior probabilities to estimate expression intensity without evaluating their performance to the ground truth [22,26]. Several studies [20,25] found that classifier margin and expression intensity were positively correlated during posed expressions. However, such correlations have typically been lower during spontaneous expressions. In a highly relevant study, Whitehill et al. [25] focused on the estimation of spontaneous smile intensity and found a high correlation between classifier margin and smile intensity on only five short video clips. Recent studies used other methods such as regression [7,11,12] and multiclass classifiers [15]. These studies have found that the predictions were typically highly correlated with expression intensity during both posed and spontaneous expressions.

Most of these previous works are limited since the majority of them focused on posed expressions, which limits the external validity and generalizability of their models. Some studies only coded expressions peak intensities, while others obtained frame-level ground truth, only for few subjects. The results reported on systems trained and tested on acted expressions might not be generalize to spontaneous ones.

Two studies are described in [10]. In the first study the authors evaluate whether two robust vision-based measures can be used to discriminate between different emotions in a dataset containing acted facial expressions under uncontrolled conditions. In the second one, they evaluate in the same dataset the accuracy of a commercially available software used for automatic emotion recognition under controlled conditions. Piana et al. [17] focus on the body movement analysis. A set of 2D and 3D features is introduced and a dictionary learning method is described to classify emotions. Preliminary results are shown to assess the importance of the studied features in solving the problem. Shan et al. [21] use the fusion of facial expressions and body gestures at the feature level and derive an "affect" space by performing Canonical Correlation Analysis. In [18], the authors apply feature extraction techniques to multi-modal audio-RGB-depth data. They compute a set of behavioral indicators that defines communicative cues coming from the fields of psychology and observational methodology. The proposed approach relies on a set of features extracted from RGB-D upper body images captured in unconstraint environment where the subjects were expressing their emotions spontaneously.

3   Methodology and Contributions

We propose in the following two methods that indicate the positive/negative emotion performed spontaneously by a single person sitting in front of a camera.

3.1   RGB-Based Approach

The main steps of this approach are divided into two stages. The first one consists in the different processing steps that allow to extract a normalized face from the input data. The second one consists in locating selected ROI from the face region and applying a specific filtering to each region to indicate the presence of a negative emotion, while the positive emotion is extracted using a neural network.

3.1.1   Image Pre-processing

The image pre-processing procedure is a very important step in the facial expression recognition task. The aim of the pre-processing phase is to obtain images that have normalized intensity, are uniform in size and shape, and depict only the face region.

A) Face detection : We use a Boosted Haar like features method. The detection of the face is performed using the Viola-Jones face detector algorithm [24] available in OpenCV library. The selected parameters achieve the best speed and performance.

B) Eye detection : We use a neural network based approach to locate the positions of pupils. We derive only the eye detection code from the STASM library [16] which is variation of Active Shape Model of Coote's implementation. However, it works better on frontal views of upright faces with neutral expressions.

C) Up-right face : We estimate the orientation of the face using the vertical positions of the two eyes. If they are not in the same position, we compute the angle between these two pupil points and correct the orientation by setting the face center as origin point and we rotate the whole frame in opposite direction. It guaranteed a frontal upright position of the face up to 30 degrees in both sideways.

D) Face normalization : We use histogram equalization to normalize image intensity by improving its contrast. It aims to eliminate light and illumination related defects from the facial area.

3.1.2 Positive/Negative Emotion Indicators Extraction

In order to detect negative emotion, we focus on the ROI located in the upper part of the face and includes the variations of AU4 of FACS where eyebrows are lowered and drawn together. We apply Gabor filter to this region of face. In the literature, 2D Gabor filters have been used for texture analysis and classification. Gabor filters have both frequency and orientation selective properties. Therefore a 2D Gabor function is composed of a sinusoidal wave of specified radial frequency which is the spacing factor between the kernels in the frequency domain and orientation which is modulated by a 2D Gaussian. Gabor representation of a face image is computed by convolving the face image I (x, y) with the Gabor filter. Majority of AUs samples associated to negative emotion face images has vertical lines above the nasal root. So, we choose vertical orientation for the Gabor filter with a frequency of $\sqrt{1.3}$, Mu equal to 0, Sigma equal to π and Nu equal to 3 as Gabor parameters. Then real and imaginary responses are added together to find the magnitude response. After a binary thresholding, the sum of the total pixels in the magnitude response of the filter, just above the nasal root is examined by a threshold value to detect a negative emotion. Brighter pixels in the magnitude responses are used as an indicator of negative emotion as depicted in the Figure 1.

In order to detect positive emotion, we use an analytic approach that performs wrapper based feature selection by exhaustive searching of all possible set of feature windows to find informative pixels. For a given emotion class, a mask is created to improve the Multilayer Perceptron (MLP) model's performance as illustrated in the Figure 1.

3.2 Depth-Based Approach

In this section we shall present a second methodology for dynamic flows analysis of depth images of the upper body in order to capture its dynamics. As stated by researchers in social psychology, the expression of the emotion by human beings is performed in different ways. In addition to verbal and facial expressions, the body motions are considered as important source of information to interpret the emotions of humans, by their peers. We propose here a geometric framework to extract the body dynamics (movements) from the depth camera observing the subject.

Formally, we propose to map the flow of T depth images $\{I^t\}_{1 \leq t \leq T}$ to a Grassmann manifold. Then, it is possible to use tools from differential geometry to quantify similarity/difference between elements and to find the most efficient way to move from one point to another (using geodesics), thus capture the

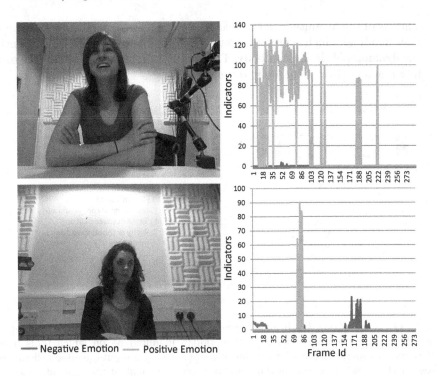

Fig. 1. Negative/Positive emotion indicators extracted from two subjects of the Cam3D dataset

dynamics. As illustrated in Figure 2, a sequence of depth images of the upper body observed by the camera is collected then organized as fragments of a fixed window size, denoted by $W(t)$. Following [23], each video fragment is mapped to a Grassmann manifold by computing the the k-dimensional subspace. When two successive elements on the Grassmann manifold are available, says x and y, we compute the the initial velocity (tangent) vector v from x towards y to characterize the body movements across the observation time. The proposed method has several benefits compared to previous descriptions as optical flow or Motion History Images [3] to capture body movements across a depth image sequence:

- Depth images acquired with MS Kinect or any other cost-effective sensor are usually noisy, of low resolution, usually returns inaccurate depth measurements, and present missing parts. This could affect negatively conventional tools to capture motions across time for example optical flow or History of Motion History. The proposed geometric framework is more robust to these factor for several reasons. The most important one is the use of a sub-space computed from a set of images instead of single image which allows to filter out the noise and handle the low resolution problem.

– The use of the magnitude of the velocity vector between points on the Grassman manifold which represent depth video fragments to capture efficiently the dynamics of the human body. This feature summarizes robustly the evolution across time of the body movements.

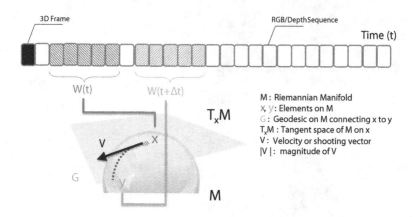

Fig. 2. Overview of our depth image approach: The flow of depth images is mapped through depth video fragments to a Riemannian manifold M on which tools from differential geometry are used to define tangent spaces, compute geodesic distances between elements and define initial velocity vector (element of the tangent space to M on x, $T_x(M)$) which allows to moves from x towards y along the geodesic path connecting them. The velocity vector will be used to capture the human body dynamics.

3.2.1 Modeling the Depth Flows on $G_{m,k}$

Before coming to the depth representation on the Grassman manifold a set of simple pre-processing steps are first applied, that we describe in the following. Given a depth video, we first separate at each frame $z = f(x, y)$ the body region from the background. Then, we reshape z to get a m-dimensional vector. A set of n successive frames, starting at a time t are considered together to form $W(t)$, a fragment of the depth sequence of size $m \times n$. From this matrix, we compute a k-dimensional subspace using the *Singular Value Decomposition* (SVD), where $k \leq n$. As a result, the depth video fragments $W(t)$ are viewed, after mapping, as elements on the Grassmann manifold $G_{m,k}$. Let X_i, $i = 1, \ldots, n$ denote n matrices of size $(m \times k)$ such that $X'X = I_k$. The rows of each X_i correspond to a low-dimensional representation of different "views" of the same object and the columns refer to the same depth pixel tracked across the observed video. Now, the depth videos are preprocessed and mapped to a Grassmann manifold of well-known geometry [5]. It is possible, using tools from differential geometry, to:

– Quantify the similarity of video fragments by interpolating between elements on $G_{m,k}$ and measuring the length of the obtained path (called geodesic path),
– Compute a sample mean of a set of elements,

- Compute the 'Energy' needed to move from an element towards another along the geodesic path connecting them,
- Model variability in a class of elements and perform fragments classification, etc.

In the following we shall recall few useful notations and relevant tools related to the geometry of the Grassmann manifold $G_{m,k}$. It is important to recall that the Grassmann manifold could be identified by a quotient manifold of the spacial orthogonal manifold by $SO(m)/SO(k) \times SO(m-k) = V_{m,k}/SO(k)$, where $V_{m,k}$ is the Stiefel manifold, the set of k-frames in $\mathbb{R}^m$, where a set of k orthonormal vectors in $\mathbb{R}^m$ is called a k-frame [5]. The Grassmann manifold $G_{m,k}$ obtained by identifying those matrices in $V_{m,k}$ whose columns span the same subspace (a quotient manifold). This quotient representation allows to extend the results of the base manifold (here $SO(m)$) such as tangent spaces and geodesics to the quotient spaces ($G_{m,k}$ in our case) [23]. Each point on $G_{m,k}$ can be represented by m-by-k matrix X such that $X^t X = I_k$.

1. **Tangent space**: To perform differential calculus on $G_{m,k}$, one needs to specify tangent space attached to it on a given point, then define an inner product. For the m-by-m identity matrix I, an element of $SO(m)$, the tangent space $T_I(SO(m))$ is the set of all m-by-m skew-symmetirc matrices [23]. For an arbitrary point $O \in SO(m)$, the tangent space at that point is obtained by a simple rotation of $T_I(SO(m))$: $T_O(SO(n)) = OX | X \in T_I(SO(m))$. For any $Y, Z \in T_O(SO(m))$ the inner product on the tangent plane $T_O(SO(m))$ is defined by $< Y, Z >= trace(YZ^T)$, where trace denotes the sum of diagonal elements. With this metric $SO(n)$ becomes a Riemannian manifold.

2. **Subspace angles**: The principal angles or canonical angles $0 \leq \theta_1 \leq \ldots \theta_m \leq \pi/2$ between the subspaces span(X) and span(Y) are defined recursively by $\cos(\theta_k) = \max\limits_{u_k \in span(X)} \max\limits_{v_k \in span(Y)} u_k' v_k$, subject to $u_k' u_k = 1, v_k' v_k = 1, u_k' u_i = 0, v_k' v_i = 0, (i = 1, \ldots, k-1)$. The principal angles can be computed from the SVD of $X'Y$ [4], $X'Y = U(\cos \Theta)V'$, where $U = [u_1 \ldots u_m]$, $V = [v_1 \ldots v_m]$, and $\cos \Theta$ is the diagonal matrix defined by:

$$\cos \Theta = diag(\cos \theta_1 \ldots \cos \theta_m)$$

3. **Geodesic distance**: The geodesic distance or the length of the minimal curve connecting span(X) and span(Y) is derived from the intrinsic geometry of Grassmann manifold. It could be expressed with the subspace angles as given by Eq. (1).

$$d(X, Y) = \left(\sum_{i=1}^{q} \theta_i^2 \right)^{1/2} = \|\Theta\|_2 \qquad (1)$$

4. **Velocity (tangent) vector**: Let $\alpha(t) : [0, 1] \to SO(m)$ a parametrized curve (or path) on $SO(m)$, then $\frac{d\alpha}{dt}$, the velocity vector at t, is an element of

the tangent space $T_{\alpha(t)}(SO(m))$. The physical interpretation of this velocity vector computed along the special case of geodesics connecting $\alpha(0)$ to $\alpha(1)$ is the energy needed to move from $\alpha(0)$ towards $\alpha(1)$ along the minimal path α.

3.2.2   Modeling the Emotional Dynamics on $G_{m,k}$

To capture the body movements, we use the notion of initial velocity vector defined for geodesic between points on the Riemannian manifold. Let $\alpha(t)$ is a constant speed geodesic starting at x and pointing towards y. Then, it is possible to compute the initial velocity v, element of $T_x(SO(m))$. Formally, $v = exp_x^{-1}(y)$ where the exp^{-1} is the inverse exponential map for which the expression is not available analytically. We use the numerical solution described in [23].

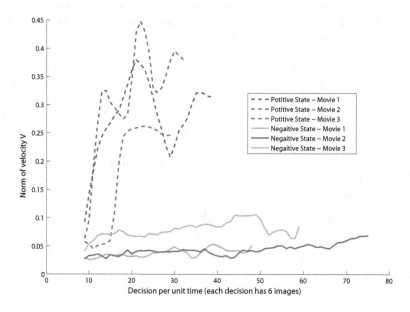

Fig. 3. Norm of velocities against time computed for three positive (dashed lines) and three negative (continuous lines) videos taken from the cam3D dataset

Accordingly, given a flow of depth images of an observed subject, we split the video to fragments of a defined window size. Then, we measure the energy needed to move from successive elements on the Grassmann manifold to describe the dynamics of the human body. More specifically, we compute the norm of the velocity vectors as features for the observed motions across time. Figure 3 shows the norm of the velocity vector against time for three positive and three negative emotional videos. It can be seen from these plots that positive emotional states are accompanied by more body movements compared to the negative emotional states. So, the values of the norm of the velocity vector across time is higher when a positive state is expressed by the subject observed by the camera. The feature vectors resulted from the previous step are feed up to a conventional classifier in order to train a classification model. In our experiments, presented in 4.2, we use the Random Forest classifier.

4 Experiments and Results

In order to evaluate the described methods, we tested them on a publicly available dataset called Cam3D [14] that records the spontaneous and natural complex mental states of different subjects using kinect. We use random forest classifier to predict the positivity and negativity of emotions.

4.1 3D Database of Spontaneous Complex Mental States

The corpus includes spontaneous facial expressions and hand gestures labelled using crowd-sourcing and is publicly available. The dataset contains a 3D multimodal corpus of 108 audio/video segments of natural complex mental states presented in [14]. The Figure 4 illustrates some examples of still images from the labelled videos.

Fig. 4. Examples of still images from the Cam3D dataset (from [14])

The dataset has been divided in four groups. The first group induce cognitive mental states : thinking, concentrating, unsure, confused and triumphant. The second group of affective states was frustrated and angry. It was ethically difficult to elicit strong negative feelings in a dyadic interaction. The third group included bored and neutral. It was also hard to elicit boredom intentionally in a dyadic interaction, so this was only attempted in the computer based session by adding a "voice calibration" task. The last group included only surprised. In the computer-based session, the computer screen flickered suddenly in the middle of the "voice calibration" task. In the dyadic interaction session, surprise was induced by flickering the lights of the room suddenly at the end of the session.

The purpose of our system is to recognize the state of an affective dimension. We are interested to detect positive/negative emotions. In order to identify the negative and positive emotions, we have used the emotion annotation and representation language (**EARL**) proposed by the Human-Machine Interaction Network on Emotion (HUMAINE) [1] that classifies 48 emotions. We use **EARL** to split the different mental states categories of Cam3D dataset into positive and negative classes.

4.2   Random Forest-Based Classifier

Upper body-based mental state classification is a binary problem which classifies the state of query movie to positive or negative. We carry out experiments with the well-known machine learning algorithm, named Random Forest. Random Forest is a set of learning method that grows a forest of classification trees based on random selected features and thresholds. To give a decision for each window of the video, the input vector is fed to each tree and each tree gives a classification result. The forest selects the result by simple majority voting. We use random forest classification since it is reported that face classification by Random Forest achieves lower error rate than some popular classifiers [13].

4.3   Experimental Results

We evaluate our approaches on the 108 videos of the Cam3D dataset. We use a 10-fold subject-independent cross-validation with Random Forest. For each round, images of some videos are randomly selected for testing, with images of remaining videos dedicated for training. For all the 10 rounds of experiments, no common subjects are used in training and testing. The input of random forest classifier is composed by the positive and negative indicators for the 2D approach where it is composed by the initial velocity descriptors for the depth image approach. The Figure 3 illustrates the comparison of the norm of the velocity vector between some negative and positive videos selected from the Cam3D dataset. Furthermore, we propose to combine both modalities by fusing their feature vectors that we feed up to RandomForest. The idea is to combine two sets of feature vectors of 2D and depth image methods and we group two sets of feature vectors into one union-vector (or a supervector).

Table 1. Comparison of the performance of 2D, depth image and RGB-D approaches using the Cam3D dataset

Approach Based	2D image	Depth image	RGB-D
Random Forest Classifier	63.00%	68.12%	**71.32%**

The Table 1 shows the results of the modalities taken individually and their combinaison. The depth-based approach (which analyze the upper body dynamics) outperforms the color-based approach (which analyzes the face). This states that the movements that exhibits the upper body are more informative than the expressions displayed by the face for spontanious emotion. Their fusion outperforms the modalities taken individually, with 71.32% classification rate, which presents a good achivement on the the Cam3D database. Recall that this database presents difficult challenges as the occlusions, various body postures, different illumination conditions, and low quality of depth images. It is clear from this experiment that the facial expressions and the body dynamics provide synchronized and complementary interpretations of the human intentions.

5   Conclusion

In this paper, we have presented approaches to analyze (1) 2D facial movies, (3) depth movies of the upper body and (3) their combinaison to estimate the complex affect state of subjects in terms of positive and negative mood. These approches have been tested on the challenging Cam3D dataset collected using Kinect sensors. When the 2D-based approach is based on Positive/Negative emotion indicators extracted from the face part of the RGB channel, the Depth-based approch uses a geometric framework able to quantify the body dynamics from the low quality depth videos. The results demonstrates that the combinaison of 2D and depth (RGB-D) outperforms the modalities taken individually. In our future work, we will focus on reducing the impact of the occlusions on the quality of the extracted descriptors and using other strategy of feature fusion of information that comes from RGB-D data.

References

1. HUMAINE Emotion Annotation and Representation Language (EARL) (June 2006). http://emotion-research.net/earl
2. Afzal, S., Robinson, P.: Natural affect data - collection & annotation in a learning context. In: Affective Computing and Intelligent Interaction and Workshops, pp. 1–7, September 2009
3. Atiqur Rahman Ahad, M., Tan, J.K., Kim, H., Ishikawa, S.: Motion history image: Its variants and applications. Mach. Vision Appl., 23(2), 255–281 (2012)
4. Björck, Å., Golub, G.H.: Numerical Methods for Computing Angles Between Linear Subspaces. Mathematics of Computation 27(123) (1973)
5. Chikuse, Y.: Statistics on Special Manifolds. Springer (February 2003)
6. Cowie, R.: Building the databases needed to understand rich, spontaneous human behaviour. In: 8th IEEE International Conference on Automatic Face Gesture Recognition, pp. 1–6, September 2008
7. Dhall, A., Goecke, R.: Group expression intensity estimation in videos via gaussian processes. In: 2012 21st International Conference on Pattern Recognition (ICPR), pp. 3525–3528. IEEE (2012)
8. Edelman, A., Arias, T.A., Smith, S.T.: The geometry of algorithms with orthogonality constraints. SIAM Journal on Matrix Analysis and Applications 20(2), 303–353 (1998)
9. Ekman, P., Friesen, W.V., Ellsworth, P.: Emotion in the Human Face. Oxford University Press (1972)
10. Antonio, D., Jáuregui, G., Martin, J.-C.: Evaluation of vision-based real-time measures for emotions discrimination under uncontrolled conditions. In: Proceedings of the 2013 on Emotion Recognition in the Wild Challenge and Workshop, EmotiW 2013, pp. 17–22. ACM, New York (2013)

11. László Jeni, A., Girard, J.M., Cohn, J.F., De La Torre, F.: Continuous au intensity estimation using localized, sparse facial feature space. In: 2013 10th IEEE International Conference and Workshops on Automatic Face and Gesture Recognition (FG), pp. 1–7. IEEE (2013)

12. Kaltwang, S., Rudovic, O., Pantic, M.: Continuous Pain Intensity Estimation from Facial Expressions. In: Bebis, G., Boyle, R., Parvin, B., Koracin, D., Fowlkes, C., Wang, S., Choi, M.-H., Mantler, S., Schulze, J., Acevedo, D., Mueller, K., Papka, M. (eds.) ISVC 2012, Part II. LNCS, vol. 7432, pp. 368–377. Springer, Heidelberg (2012)

13. Kouzani, A., Nahavandi, S., Khoshmanesh, K.: Face classification by a random forest. In: IEEE Region 10 Conference: TENCON (2007)

14. Mahmoud, M., Baltrušaitis, T., Robinson, P., Riek, L.D.: 3D Corpus of Spontaneous Complex Mental States. In: D'Mello, S., Graesser, A., Schuller, B., Martin, J.-C. (eds.) ACII 2011, Part I. LNCS, vol. 6974, pp. 205–214. Springer, Heidelberg (2011)

15. Mahoor, M.H., Cadavid, S., Messinger, D.S., Cohn, J.F.: A framework for automated measurement of the intensity of non-posed facial action units. In: IEEE Computer Society Conference on Computer Vision and Pattern Recognition Workshops, CVPR Workshops 2009, pp. 74–80. IEEE (2009)

16. Milborrow, S., Nicolls, F.: Locating facial features with an extended active shape model. In: 10th European Conference on Computer Vision (2008)

17. Piana, S., Staglianò, A., Camurri, A., Odone, F.: A set of full-body movement features for emotion recognition to help children affected by autism spectrum condition. In: IDGEI International Workshop (2013)

18. Ponce-López, V., Escalera, S., Baró, X.: Multi-modal social signal analysis for predicting agreement in conversation settings. In: Proceedings of the 15th ACM on International Conference on Multimodal Interaction, pp. 495–502. ACM (2013)

19. Rozin, P., Cohen, A.B.: High Frequency of Facial Expressions Corresponding to Confusion, Concentration, and Worry in an Analysis of Naturally Occurring Facial Expressions of Americans. Emotion **3**(1), 68–75 (2003)

20. Savran, A., Sankur, B., Taha Bilge, M.: Regression-based intensity estimation of facial action units. Image and Vision Computing, 30(10), 774–784 (2012). 3D Facial Behaviour Analysis and Understanding

21. Shan, C., Gong, S., McOwan, P.W.: Beyond facial expressions: Learning human emotion from body gestures. In: BMVC, pp. 1–10 (2007)

22. Shimada, K., Noguchi, Y., Kuria, T.: Fast and robust smile intensity estimation by cascaded support vector machines. International Journal of Computer Theory & Engineering 5(1) (2013)

23. Turaga, P.K., Veeraraghavan, A., Srivastava, A., Chellappa, R.: Statistical computations on grassmann and stiefel manifolds for image and video-based recognition. IEEE Trans. Pattern Anal. Mach. Intell. **33**(11), 2273–2286 (2011)

24. P. Viola and M. J. Jones. Rapid object detection using a boosted cascade of simple features. In: International Conference on Computer Vision and Pattern Recognition (CVPR) (2001)

25. Whitehill, J., Littlewort, G., Fasel, I., Bartlett, M., Movellan, J.: Toward practical smile detection. IEEE Transactions on Pattern Analysis and Machine Intelligence **31**(11), 2106–2111 (2009)

26. Yang, P., Liu, Q., Metaxas D.N.: Rankboost with l1 regularization for facial expression recognition and intensity estimation. In: ICCV, pp. 1018–1025 (2009)

Friendly Faces:
Weakly Supervised Character Identification

Matthew Marter$^{(\boxtimes)}$, Simon Hadfield, and Richard Bowden

CVSSP, University of Surrey, Surrey, UK
{m.marter,s.hadfield,r.bowden}@surrey.ac.uk

Abstract. This paper demonstrates a novel method for automatically discovering and recognising characters in video without any labelled examples or user intervention. Instead weak supervision is obtained via a rough script-to-subtitle alignment. The technique uses pose invariant features, extracted from detected faces and clustered to form groups of co-occurring characters. Results show that with 9 characters, 29% of the closest exemplars are correctly identified, increasing to 50% as additional exemplars are considered.

1 Introduction

This paper presents an approach to weakly supervised character identification from video footage using subtitle and script information as weak supervision in a facial clustering process. This is challenging as the the annotation gained from scripts and subtitles is a weak verbal commentary and the pose, expression and lighting of characters is highly variable. To overcome these problems we present an approach which incorporates both subtitle and shot boundary detection into a script alignment process which gives accurate start and end times for each scene. The script also indicates which characters are present within each scene. By automatically detecting faces throughout the video, accurately regressing facial features and then using these facial features in an unsupervised clustering process, individuals can be identified without user intervention. The script information is used as weak supervision in this clustering process to identify the likelihood of characters over subsets of frames. We demonstrate a completely unsupervised approach to character identification and show results on the popular American sitcom "Friends" (See Fig 1).

The remainder of this paper is structured as follows. In section 2 we discuss relevant related work in the areas of script alignment, character identification and shot boundary detection. In section 3 we present the proposed methodology with scene identification and timing described in section 3.1, facial feature detection and extraction described in section 3.2 and the facial clustering process described in section 3.3. Section 4 describes results and conclusions and future work are discussed in section 5.

© Springer International Publishing Switzerland 2015
Q. Ji et al. (Eds.): FFER 2014, LNCS 8912, pp. 121–132, 2015.
DOI: 10.1007/978-3-319-13737-7_11

Fig. 1. Example faces from Friends opening sequence

2   Related Work

Computer vision has seen the use of video footage increase in previous years and areas such as action recognition have moved away from staged datasets such as KTH [29] and Weizmann [2], which are generally considered "solved" with many techniques reporting performance of 95% or more. As a result, recent action recognition datasets have been concerned with action recognition "in the wild", dealing with unconstrained variations in location, lighting, camera angle, actor and action style. Alternative means for obtaining data have been explored, including videos obtained from youtube [17] and clips extracted from commercially available films (e.g. "Hollywood" [15], "Hollywood 2" [19] and "Hollywood 3D"[12]).

The size of the Hollywood 2 dataset was facilitated by the automated extraction process employed by Marszalek *et al.* [19]. Such techniques offer ease in data collection and rely on the extraction of time stamped subtitles from the film. These subtitles are then aligned with film scripts, which describe the behaviour of the actors in addition to dialogue.

Perhaps one of the earliest attempts to use script information was the work of Everingham et al.[8][9]. Everingham used the subtitles to provide timing information by matching it with the dialogue in the scripts. When there are inconsistencies with the script and subtitle information, dynamic time warping is used to find the best alignment. When subtitle information is either not available or there are scenes without dialogue, other methods need to be used to provide alignment information. Sankar et al.[28] use a combination of location recognition, facial recognition and speech-to-text to align scripts when subtitles are not available. However, the approach requires manual labelling of characters and location information was hard-coded to repetitive use of stock footage. Subtitles have also been used as weak supervision in learning sign [4,6,26].

Subtitles only provide timing information for dialogue. However, identifying shots within a video can help to identify when a scene containing dialogue might start or end. A shot in a video sequence is a group of continuous frames between edits. The edits can take various forms such as fades or abrupt transitions. To be able to learn about scenes, a video must first be divided into shots. Hanjalic[13] defines the problem of Shot Boundary Detection (SBD) as finding discontinuities in the feature distance between frames. Many different feature types have been used for SBD including: Pixel differences[35], Colour histograms[20], tracking of features[10] and mutual information[5]. Yuan et al.[34] try to provide a formal framework for SBD and review many existing techniques while suggesting optimal criteria for the different sections of the framework. To take advantage of existing information, Patel et al.[25] use the motion vectors from the video compression to detect cuts. Due to the large number of approaches available, there have been many survey papers such as Boreczky and Rowe[3] and Smeaton et al.[30]. Boeczky and Rowe find that, in general, the approaches based on region-based comparisons and motion vectors worked better and simpler algorithms out performed more complex ones. Smeaton et al. found that there was usually very little difference in performance between the top approaches and shot cut performance is still a lot higher than gradual transitions.

This work integrates shot cut detection into the script-subtitle alignment process to provide accurate scene level annotation. We then use character information from the scripts as weak supervision to automatically identify characters by clustering their facial descriptors.

3   Methodology

Figure 2 gives an overview of the approach. Firstly the subtitles are extracted from the video along with the shot boundaries which are detected in the video footage. Fuzzy text matching is used to match the dialogue in the script with that of the subtitles and scene boundaries are constrained to only occur on shot boundaries. This extends the dialogue timing to give the start and end times of scenes. Using the time aligned script, all scenes for each character are identified along with the presence of other characters in the same scenes. This is passed

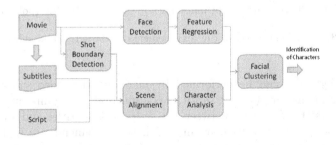

Fig. 2. Character identification framework

to the clustering process along with the face descriptors for the corresponding frames. Face descriptors are extracted from detected faces by regressing the facial pose and extracting SIFT features around the contour of the face. Unsupervised clustering then provides sets of visually similar face descriptors which are assigned identities from the script.

3.1   Scene Identification

Television and film scripts contain the details for the scenes within a video sequence. There is a standardised format for scripts and their contents. This format specifies the location in which the scene occurs, editorial information for the shots, a description of the activities and actions occurring within the scene and the dialogue spoken by the characters. The location information is contained within the "slug lines" which state if the scene is exterior or interior, where it is and the time of day it occurs. The script Γ contains text elements t, $\Gamma = t_{0...n}$. The scenes within a script are a subset of the script. The scene boundaries A are defined as $A \subset \Gamma$. Equation 1 defines the text scene Σ^T as the text between the scene boundaries in the script,

$$\Sigma^T{}_j = \{j | A_{k-1} < j < A_k\}. \tag{1}$$

The script does not, however, contain any information about the timing of the scenes within the video. To use the scripts as annotation, the contents of the video and the script need to be aligned.

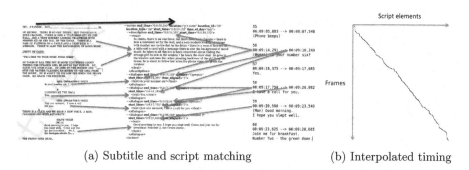

(a) Subtitle and script matching   (b) Interpolated timing

Fig. 3. Alignment between the text elements in the script and subtitles

Initial alignment can be performed by matching the video subtitles with the dialogue in the scripts. The subtitles contain text and timing information. Figure 3 shows the alignment between the script and subtitles and an example of how the script and subtitles are matched. Black elements are well aligned, blue elements are interpolated and orange elements are when multiple script elements occur simultaneously. The subtitles sub have text, $sub^t = t$, as well as start frames, sub^s, and end frames, sub^e. Fuzzy matching between subtitle text and script text is used to assign start and end frames to script text as in equation 2. This gives us the images that belong to a scene Σ^I,

$$\Sigma^I{}_j = \{j | \text{argmin}(sub^s) < j < \text{argmax}(sub^e) \text{ and } sub^t \in \Sigma^T{}_j\}. \tag{2}$$

Scene Boundary Refinement. The frames which occur between subtitles are ill-defined. A scene can contain many shots and a scene cannot change during a shot. Our method requires that we divide the video into shots so that they can be matched to scenes. We use a shot boundary detection method based on calculating the homography from one frame to the next. We trigger a shot boundary when the homography between shots is invalid.

A video consists of a set of images, $I = i_{1...n}$. The set of shot boundaries (SB) is where the homography ($h_{j,j+1}$) between consecutive images (i_j and i_{j+1}) leads to a transformed image with an area smaller than a threshold (t),

$$SB = \left\{ j \left| \frac{|h_{j,j+1}(i_j)|}{|i_j|} < t \right. \right\}. \tag{3}$$

A particular shot (S_k) is defined as the set of frames which between 2 consecutive shot boundaries (SB_k and SB_{k+1}),

$$S_k = \{i_j | SB_k < j < SB_{k+1}\}. \tag{4}$$

We define the scenes Σ^S using the shots that belong to them,

$$\Sigma^S{}_k = \left\{ \bigcup_j S_j | S_j \bigcap \Sigma^I{}_k \neq \emptyset \right\}. \tag{5}$$

This gives us all the shots belonging to a scene so that frames which occur after or before a subtitle are also included. This avoids missing face candidates that occur without dialogue.

3.2 Face Extraction

Cootes suggested learning a simple linear mapping between facial image intensity difference and the pose of an Active Appearance Model (AAM) in 1998 [7]. Similar ideas have since been applied to tracking rigid objects [14][21] as well as using more complex, non-linear mappings in regression tracking [32]. Zimmerman et al. proposed the idea of a sequential linear predictor and this idea was applied to facial feature regression by Ong and Bowden [23][24], whose sequential and hierarchical linear predictors can be trained using Monte-Carlo sampling to accurately track facial features in real-time. The same principle was adopted by Xiong and De la Torre [33] to regress from SIFT [18] features rather than image intensities. Both approaches use a simple cascade of sequential linear mappings but SIFT gives better person independence in the regression process. Another

(a) Facial Landmarks   (b) Regressed Landmarks   (c) Sequential Regression

Fig. 4. Facial Feature Regression

difference between Ong and Xiong is the latter regress all feature points in a single regressor which captures the motion dependency of the features unlike Ong who treat each facial feature as independent. We combine these ideas to train a cascade of linear predictors that regress facial position from SIFT features extracted at each facial landmark.

Given a set of face images $d_i \in D$ with associated facial landmarks $x_i \in X$, the objective is to find a mapping H that can predict the displacement of the landmarks δx such that $\delta x = H\phi(x)$. The image observation, $\phi(x) \in \mathbb{R}^{nm+1}$, is a 6733 dimensional concatenated SIFT vector where $n = 99$ is the dimension of a SIFT descriptor after projection through PCA, $m = |x|/2$ is the number of facial landmarks (in our case 68) and a single dimension is added for the bias term in linear regression.

To learn H, a training set of random displacements $T \in \mathbb{R}^{(|x| \times r|X|)}$ is extracted by randomly offsetting the model from the true face location and recording the displacements. For each displacement the image observations are compiled into $\Phi \in \mathbb{R}^{(|\phi| \times r|X|)}$ where $r = 10$ is the number of random offsets per image.

H is then calculated as the least squares solution $H = T(\Phi\Phi^T)^{-1}$. As a single linear mapping is insufficient to model the complexities of a highly deformable object like a face, a sequence of regressors is used where $\delta x^i = H^i \phi(x_0 + \delta x^{i-1})$.

We train our facial regressor using 5691 example images taken from the *300 Faces in-the-wild* challenge dataset (300-W) [27]. These images are annotated using the Multi-PIE [11] 68 point mark up shown in Figure 4a. The full dataset consists of consistent re-annotations for LFPW [1], AFW [36], HELEN [16] and XM2VTS [22]. We refrain from using the additional 135 IBUG images and the testing subsets of the aforementioned datasets which are retained for internal validation e.g. regressor convergence during training.

Figure 4a shows the 68 landmark points used in our regression and Figure 4b the result of applying the learnt regressor to a sample static image. At runtime, a Viola Jones boosted face detector [31] is applied to each frame. Following non maximal suppression, the regressor is independently applied at each positive detection using the mean face $x_0 = \frac{1}{|x|}\sum_{\forall x_i \in X} x_i$ as the initial estimate as was used during training. The initial face estimate is scaled and translated to the detected face region and the SIFT features are set at one tenth of the face scale which translates to roughly half the size of an eye. The regressor typically converges onto the face using 4-5 linear predictors in the sequential cascade.

Figure 4c shows the process of regression for each regressor in the cascade starting from a mean face (dark) to final regression (yellow). An example of regressing multiple faces from a frame taken from Friends is shown in Figure 1.

3.3 Face Clustering

To allow us to name the faces we have extracted, we can cluster the face descriptors and label them with character names from the script. To avoid clustering all of the face descriptors at once, which could cause less pure clusters, we divide the descriptors into subsets that contains all occurences of a certain character. For each scene, the characters Π_k are defined using the characters z present in $\Sigma^S{}_k$. The set of all the characters in the episode, Z, is defined by $Z = \bigcup_k \Pi_k$. With the script aligned to the video, we can use the scene boundaries to work out the frames and face descriptors belonging to these scenes. This gives us a matrix of images with character co-occurrence,

$$\mathbf{E}_{xy} = \{i | i \in \Sigma^S{}_z \text{ and } z_x \in \Pi_z \text{ and } z_y \in \Pi_z\}. \tag{6}$$

We can then normalise by the number of frames each character is in,

$$\bar{\mathbf{E}}_{jk} = \frac{|\mathbf{E}_{jk}|}{\sum_l |\mathbf{E}_{jl}|}. \tag{7}$$

For each character z_k we perform k-means on the descriptors for all face candidates Υ_k. The co-occurence of characters is used to reduce the number of characters present in the input to the k-means. The face candidates are obtained by,

$$\Upsilon_k = \{v^F | v^F \in \Sigma^S{}_j \text{ and } z_k \in \Pi_j\}. \tag{8}$$

The number of clusters p is calculated from the total number of characters present in the scenes using,

$$p_i = |\{\mathbf{E}_{jk} \neq 0\}|. \tag{9}$$

We expect that the face descriptors will be clustered into the characters. The cluster centres C are found by the k-means algorithm,

$$C_k = \text{kmeans}(\Upsilon_k; p_k). \tag{10}$$

We now have the the clusters of face candidates but we don't know which characters belong to each cluster. To overcome this problem we create a histogram of the number of face descriptors belonging to each cluster. The histogram M_{jk} is calculated by,

$$M_{jk} = \frac{\left|\left\{v | v \in \Upsilon_j \text{ where } \arg\min_l \left(|v - C_l|^2\right) = k\right\}\right|}{|\Upsilon_j|}. \tag{11}$$

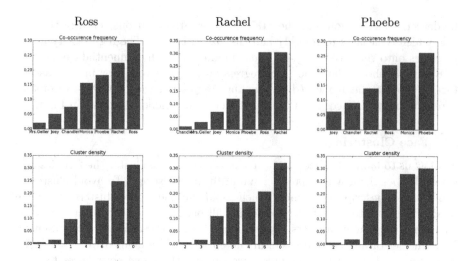

Fig. 5. Comparison of cluster density and co-occurrence frequency after identity assignment, for the 3 most common characters

To match the labels from the co-occurrence histogram to the membership histogram, we re-order the membership histogram to find the minimum χ^2 distance. We expect the largest cluster to correspond to the character themselves as they would be present the most often within their scenes. This relies on characters appearing separately from other characters in different scenes.

4   Results

We evaluated the proposed technique on a dataset of approximately 35,000 images, obtained form the TV sitcom "Friends". This program is ideal for examining the approach, as the large cast of "main" (i.e. re-occurring and named) characters, makes the task especially challenging. In addition, scripts are easily obtainable for the series, and the large amount of dialogue facilitates the accurate subtitle-to-script alignment. The total number of named characters present in the relevant scripts is 9, with co-occurrences spread across 14 different scenes.

From the dataset, around 20,000 face descriptors are extracted. After partitioning based on character co-occurrence as described in section 3.3, each character had on average of 6,830 face candidates.

4.1   Cluster Feasibility

In order to assign identities, we assume that the density of the clusters relates to the frequency of character co-occurrences. In order to evaluate this assumption figure 5 compares histograms for the 3 most commonly occurring characters in the dataset.

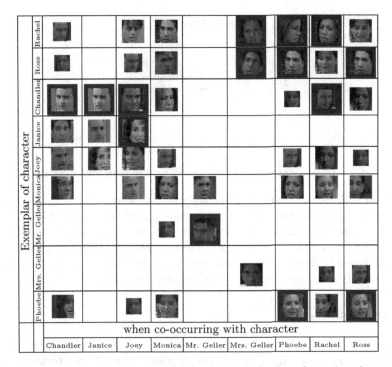

Fig. 6. Character co-occurrence matrix **E**, represented using the assigned exemplars. Exemplars with a blue border are correctly identified. Gaps indicate pairs of characters which never co-occur within the dataset. Roughly one third of cluster exemplars have had the correct identity assigned.

It can be seen that, in general, cluster density correlates well with character co-occurrence frequency, meaning that the assumption used for identity assignment is likely a valid one. There are some inconsistencies, particularly with minor characters, as they tend to talk (and be visible) less often, even when they are technically present in the scene. Thus the cluster density of the smallest clusters is generally somewhat lower than what we would expect from the script.

4.2   Character Identification

It is extremely time-consuming to manually annotate the identity of tens of thousands of face images. Avoiding this task is one of the primary motivations for our automatic data-driven approach. As such, we evaluate the technique in terms of "character exemplars". For each cluster with an assigned identity, we extract the face candidate closest to the cluster centre, and record whether this exemplar belongs to the assigned character. These exemplars are shown in figure 6 for the full co-occurrence matrix **E**. Blue borders indicate exemplars with correctly assigned identities.

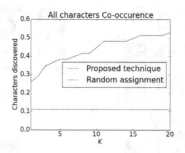

Fig. 7. Accuracy of identity assignment for the K-nearest exemplars

Overall 29% of the exemplars are assigned the correct identity. This is 2.5 times the accuracy achievable by random assignment, indicating that even the weak supervision provided by script co-occurrences, can be hugely beneficial.

We extend this evaluation to look at the the accuracy of the K-nearest exemplars, as shown in figure 7. If we examine up to the top 20 exemplars, we are able to identify more than 50% of the characters correctly.

5   Conclusions

In this paper, we have introduced an approach to identify characters in broadcast footage, without any manual intervention. Instead the technique uses weak supervision from script and subtitle alignments, to estimate character co-occurrences.

Face candidates were extracted, and described in terms of facial landmarks to mitigate pose variation. Modes in the face data were then estimated, and the density of these modes was used to assign character identities, by comparison to the expected co-occurrence rates. The technique was evaluated by examining the "exemplars" of these modes, 29% of which had the correct identity assigned (2.5 times the baseline from random assignment). Accuracy increased to over 50% when examining the top 20 exemplars per mode

In the future it would be interesting to investigate co-clustering techniques to collate character identity information across the rows of the co-occurrences. Using different clustering techniques that don't assume spherical clusters such as GMMs should allow for better modelling of the distribution of characters as well as using more clusters than there are characters. The use of the actual speaking times from the subtitles could also be used to further improve performance.

Acknowledgments. This work was supported by the EPSRC project "Learning to Recognise Dynamic Visual Content from Broadcast Footage" (EP/I011811/1).

References

1. Belhumeur, P., Jacobs, D., Kriegman, D., Kumar, N.: Localizing parts of faces using a consensus of exemplars. In: 2011 IEEE Conference on Computer Vision and Pattern Recognition (CVPR), pp. 545–552, June 2011

2. Blank, M., Gorelick, L., Shechtman, E., Irani, M., Basri, R.: Actions as space-time shapes. In: Proc. ICCV (2005)
3. Boreczky, J.S., Rowe, L.A.: Comparison of video shot boundary detection techniques. Journal of Electronic Imaging (1996)
4. Buehler, P., Everingham, M., Zisserman, A.: Learning sign language by watching tv (using weakly aligned subtitles. In: Computer Vision and Pattern Recognition (2009)
5. Cernekova, Z., Nikou, C., Pitas, I.: Shot detection in video sequences using entropy based metrics. In: Proc. ICIP (2002)
6. Cooper, H., Bowden, R.: Learning signs from subtitles: A weakly supervised approach to sign language recognition. In: IEEE Conference on Computer Vision and Pattern Recognition, CVPR 2009, pp. 2568–2574. IEEE (2009)
7. Cootes, T.F., Edwards, G.J., Taylor, C.J.: Active Appearance Models. In: Burkhardt, H., Neumann, B. (eds.) ECCV 1998. LNCS, vol. 1407, pp. 484–498. Springer, Heidelberg (1998)
8. Everingham, M., Sivic, J., Zisserman, A.: "Hello! My name is... Buffy" - automatic naming of characters in TV video. In: Proc. BMVC (2006)
9. Everingham, M., Sivic, J., Zisserman, A.: Taking the bite out of automatic naming of characters in TV video. Image and Vision Computing (2009)
10. Gao, X., Li, J., Shi, Y.: A Video Shot Boundary Detection Algorithm Based on Feature Tracking. In: Wang, G.-Y., Peters, J.F., Skowron, A., Yao, Y. (eds.) RSKT 2006. LNCS (LNAI), vol. 4062, pp. 651–658. Springer, Heidelberg (2006)
11. Gross, R., Matthews, I., Cohn, J., Kanade, T., Baker, S.: Multi-pie. Image Vision Comput. 28(5), 807–813 (2010). http://dx.doi.org/10.1016/j.imavis.2009.08.002
12. Hadfield, S., Bowden, R.: Hollywood 3D: Recognizing actions in 3D natural scenes. In: Proc. CVPR (2013)
13. Hanjalic, A.: Shot-boundary detection: unraveled and resolved? Circuits and Systems for Video Technology (2002)
14. Jurie, F., Dhome, M.: Real time robust template matching. In: BMVC (2002)
15. Laptev, I., Marszalek, M., Schmid, C., Rozenfeld, B.: Learning realistic human actions from movies. In: Proc. CVPR (2008)
16. Le, V., Brandt, J., Lin, Z., Bourdev, L., Huang, T.S.: Interactive Facial Feature Localization. In: Fitzgibbon, A., Lazebnik, S., Perona, P., Sato, Y., Schmid, C. (eds.) ECCV 2012, Part III. LNCS, vol. 7574, pp. 679–692. Springer, Heidelberg (2012)
17. Liu, J., Luo, J., Shah, M.: Recognizing realistic actions from videos in the wild. In: Proc. CVPR (2009)
18. Lowe, D.G.: Distinctive image features from scale-invariant keypoints. IJCV (2004)
19. Marszalek, M., Laptev, I., Schmid, C.: Actions in context. In: Proc. CVPR (2009)
20. Mas, J., Fernandez, G.: Video shot boundary detection based on color histogram. Notebook Papers TRECVID 2003 (2003)
21. Matas, J., Zimmermann, K., Svoboda, T., Hilton, A.: Learning efficient linear predictors for motion estimation. In: Comp. Vis. Graphics and Image Proc. (2006)
22. Messer, K., Matas, J., Kittler, J., Lttin, J., Maitre, G.: Xm2vtsdb: The extended m2vts database. In: Second International Conference on Audio and Video-based Biometric Person Authentication, pp. 72–77 (1999)
23. Ong, E.J., Bowden, R.: Robust facial feature tracking using shape-constrained multiresolution-selected linear predictors. PAMI (2011)
24. Ong, E.J., Lan, Y., Theobald, B., Harvey, R., Bowden, R.: Robust facial feature tracking using selected multi-resolution linear predictors. In: 2009 IEEE 12th International Conference on Computer Vision, pp. 1483–1490. IEEE (2009)

25. Patel, N.V., Sethi, I.K.: Compressed video processing for cut detection. In: Proc. Vision, Image and Signal Processing (1996)
26. Pfister, T., Charles, J., Zisserman, A.: Large-scale learning of sign language by watching tv (using co-occurrences). In: British Machine Vision Conference (BMVC) (2013)
27. Sagonas, C., Tzimiropoulos, G., Zafeiriou, S., Pantic, M.: 300 faces in-the-wild challenge: The first facial landmark localization challenge. In: 2013 IEEE International Conference on Computer Vision Workshops (ICCVW), pp. 397–403, December 2013
28. Sankar, P., Jawahar, C.V., Zisserman, A.: Subtitle-free movie to script alignment. In: Proc. BMVC (2009)
29. Schuldt, C., Laptev, I., Caputo, B.: Recognizing human actions: a local SVM approach. In: Proc. ICPR (2004)
30. Smeaton, A.F., Over, P., Doherty, A.R.: Video shot boundary detection: Seven years of trecvid activity. CVIU (2010)
31. Viola, P., Jones, M.: Rapid object detection using a boosted cascade of simple features (2001)
32. Williams, O., Blake, A., Cipolla, R.: A sparse probabilistic learning algorithm for real-time tracking. In: Proc. ICCV (2003)
33. Xuehan, X., De la Torre, F.: Supervised descent method and its application to face alignment. In: Proc. CVPR (2013)
34. Yuan, J., Wang, H., Xiao, L., Zheng, W., Li, J., Lin, F., Zhang, B.: A formal study of shot boundary detection. Circuits and Systems for Video Technology (2007)
35. Zhang, H., Kankanhalli, A., Smoliar, S.W.: Automatic partitioning of full-motion video. Multimedia Systems (1993)
36. Zhu, X., Ramanan, D.: Face detection, pose estimation, and landmark localization in the wild. In: 2012 IEEE Conference on Computer Vision and Pattern Recognition (CVPR), pp. 2879–2886, June 2012

A Comparative Evaluation of Regression Learning Algorithms for Facial Age Estimation

Carles Fernández[1], Ivan Huerta[2](✉), and Andrea Prati[2]

[1] Herta Security, Pau Claris 165 4-B, 08037 Barcelona, Spain
carles.fernandez@hertasecurity.com
[2] DPDCE, University IUAV, Santa Croce 1957, 30135 Venice, Italy
{huertacasado,aprati}@iuav.it

Abstract. The problem of automatic age estimation from facial images poses a great number of challenges: uncontrollable environment, insufficient and incomplete training data, strong person-specificity, and high within-range variance, among others. These difficulties have made researchers of the field propose complex and strongly hand-crafted descriptors, which make it difficult to replicate and compare the validity of posterior classification and regression schemes. We present a practical evaluation of four machine learning regression techniques from some of the most representative families in age estimation: *kernel techniques, ensemble learning, neural networks*, and *projection algorithms*. Additionally, we propose the use of simple HOG descriptors for robust age estimation, which achieve comparable performance to the state-of-the-art, without requiring piecewise facial alignment through tens of landmarks, nor fine-tuned and specific modeling of facial aging, nor additional demographic annotations such as gender or ethnicity. By using HOG descriptors, we discuss the benefits and drawbacks among the four learning algorithms. The accuracy and generalization of each regression technique is evaluated through cross-validation and cross-database validation over two large databases, MORPH and FRGC.

Keywords: Age estimation · Support Vector Regression · SVM · Random Forest · Multilayer Neural Networks · Regularized Canonical Correlation Analysis · CCA · HOG

1 Introduction

Automatically conducting human age estimation from facial images can be valuable for a number of applications, including advanced video surveillance and biometrics [3,8]; demographic statistics collection; business intelligence and customer profiling for targeted advertisements; and search optimization in large databases, to list some. Unfortunately, this problem has historically been one of the most challenging within the field of facial analysis. Some of the reasons are the uncontrollable nature of the aging process, the strong specificity to the personal traits of each individual [19], high variance of observations within the

© Springer International Publishing Switzerland 2015
Q. Ji et al. (Eds.): FFER 2014, LNCS 8912, pp. 133–144, 2015.
DOI: 10.1007/978-3-319-13737-7_12

same age range, and the fact that it is very troublesome to gather complete and sufficient data to train accurate models [4].

The process of collecting quality age-annotated samples is difficult, and has often resulted in very limited and strongly skewed databases. This is especially disadvantageous for applications like video surveillance and forensics, which need to work correctly when facing unknown subjects and a lack of any additional cues. In these cases, the availability of large databases like MORPH [16] and FRGC [15] offers a great opportunity to make advances in the field. Keeping in mind that any training data set which is representative of the whole population cannot exist, the only viable option is to develop methods that are able to exploit large databases in order to gain substantial generalization capabilities. With these premises, this study includes the following contributions:

- A comparative evaluation of four of the most prominent machine learning regression techniques that have been typically applied to the problem of age estimation: *Support Vector Regression* (SVR), *Multilayer Neural Networks* (MNN), *Random Forests* (RF), and *Canonical Correlation Analysis* (CCA).
- The first attempt to use *Histograms of Oriented Gradients* [2] as a visual descriptor for age estimation. In our study, and compared to usual features, HOG benefits from being much faster to compute, standard, and easily replicable, besides offering very similar performance to the state-of-the-art.
- A baseline proposal for incorporating cross-database validation methodologies in order to test the generalization of an approach. To this end, we also propose the use of the large FRGC database, which has not received much attention in the past for age estimation purposes.

The paper is structured as follows: the next section reports and comments on previous works on age estimation. The proposed approach and methodology is described in Section 3. Section 4 analyzes current available age databases, describes the extensive experimentation carried out, and analyzes the obtained results. Finally, Section 5 draws some conclusions and gives hints for further research.

2   Related Work

The first works and databases on automatic age estimation from digital images started appearing in the early 2000s [9–11]. Nonetheless, research in the field has experienced a renewed interest from 2006 on, since the availability of large databases like MORPH-Album 2 [16], which increased by $55\times$ the amount of real age-annotated data with respect to traditional age databases. Next, we summarize the most successful descriptors and techniques that have been recently evaluated with this database.

Existing works on age estimation can be categorized by their choice of feature and classification scheme. Regarding visual features, shape and appearance models such as ASM (Active Shape Model) and AAM (Active Appearance Model) have been some of the primary cues used to model aging patterns [1,4,5,9]. Such statistical models capture the main modes of variation in shape and intensity observed in a set of faces, and allow face signatures based on such characterizations to be encoded.

Bio-Inspired Features (BIF) [17] and its derivations have been consistently used for age estimation in the last years [4, 8]. These feed-forward models consist of a number of layers intertwining convolutionally and pooling processes. First, an input image is mapped to a higher-dimensional space by convoluting it with a bank of multi-scale and multi-orientation Gabor filters. Later, a pooling step downscales the results with a non-linear reduction, typically a MAX or STD operation, progressively encoding the results into a vector signature. In [13], the authors carefully design a two-layer simplification of this model for age estimation by manually setting the number of bands and orientations for convolution and pooling. Such features are also used in their posterior works [6, 7].

With regards to the learning algorithm, Support Vector Machines (SVM) have commonly been used for age classification and regression, as in [13]. A binary decision tree with SVMs at each node is proposed in [8]. Age ranges are coarsely assigned, and later are more precisely estimated by Support Vector Regressors (SVR) at the leaves. In [1], a particular ranking formulation of support vectors, OHRank, is used. The approach uses cost-sensitive aggregation to estimate ordinal hyperplanes (OH) and ranks them according to the relative order of ages. In this paper AAM features are used. In [19], the author employs a similar ranking technique called MFOR.

There have been previous proposals training neural networks, which are able to learn complex mappings and deal with outliers, for age estimation. In [9], AAM-encoded face parameters are used as an input for the supervised training of a neural network with a hidden layer. In this case, models were trained uniquely from 200 color images, and the number of AAM-model parameters was restricted to 22. More recently, the authors of [4] tackle age estimation as a discrete classification problem using 70 classes, one for each age. The best algorithm proposed in this work (CPNN - Conditional Probability Neural Network) consists of a three-layered neural network, in which the input to the network includes both BIF features x and a numerical value for age y, and the output neuron is a single value of the conditional probability density function $p(y|x)$.

Although ensemble learning methods have not been extensively used in the field, they are particularly suitable for environments with high-dimensional features and strongly skewed data. An approach based on Random Forests (RF) over anthropometric measurements is presented in [12]. A collection of 11K simple features such as distances and area ratios are extracted from the facial mesh derived from 68 fine-annotated fiducial markers, and directly fed to the forest. The approach is tested using the subset of 710 face images from FG-NET that are between 0 and 20 years old.

Partial Least Squares (PLS) and Canonical Correlation Analysis (CCA), along with their regularized and kernelized versions, are increasingly being used in the field of age estimation [6, 7]. These subspace learning algorithms were originally conceived to model the compatibility between two multidimensional

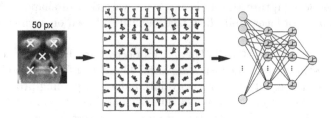

Fig. 1. The proposed study evaluates four machine learning regression techniques, all of them fed with histograms of gradients extracted from 50×50 pixel aligned images. A schematic example is shown here for the case of neural networks.

variables. PLS uses latent variables to learn a new space in which such variables have maximum correlation, whereas CCA finds basis vectors such that the projections of the two variables using these vectors are maximally correlated to each other. Both techniques have been adapted for label regression. To the best of our knowledge, the best current result over MORPH is achieved by combining BIF features with kernel CCA [7], although in that case the size of training folds is limited to 10K samples due to computational limitations.

Our experiments demonstrate that a single-scale HOG descriptor is sufficiently expressive to compare with the performance of complex, fine-tuned features such as BIF; and that alignment through 5 fiducial points results in comparable age estimation performance to precise alignment achieved through ASM/AAM fitting, which use approximately 70 landmarks. Additionally, our results show that the common strategy of partitioning age into ranges is unnecessary, since a single output neuron is able to act as an effective regressor. Posing age estimation purely as a regression problem not only simplifies the formulation, but additionally provides more accurate results when using a proper descriptor.

3   Methodology

In order to compare the performance of machine learning regression techniques in the field of age estimation, we have chosen a representative algorithm from each of four families that are conventionally used: a *Support Vector Regressor* from the kernel family, a *Multilayer Neural Network* from the neural network family, a *Random Forest* from the ensemble learning family, and a *regularized Canonical Correlation Analysis* from the projection family. These techniques are described next.

Preprocessing. In general, existing works tackle the problem of age estimation with visual features that are either complex and fine-tuned (e.g., BIF), or require precise statistical models involving tens of facial landmarks for accurate alignment (e.g., ASM or AAM models). As opposed to this, the four chosen learning algorithms will be evaluated with single-scale HOG visual descriptors after a 5-landmark alignment, see Figure 1. Histograms of Oriented Gradients (HOG) [2] have been largely used as robust visual descriptors in many computer vision applications related to object detection and recognition, due to their expressiveness, fast computation, compactness, and invariance to misalignment and monotonic illumination changes.

The facial region of each image has been extracted with the face detector described in [14]. Unlike previous approaches, we do not rely on precisely aligned appearance models. The relative alignment invariance of HOG allows us to require only five landmarks. The fiducial markers corresponding to the eye centers, nose tip and mouth corners have been obtained using the convolutional neural network for face alignment presented in [18]. The aligned version of each detected face is obtained by a non-reflective similarity image transformation that yields an optimal least-square correspondence between the set of fiducial points and the target locations, in which eye centers and mouth corners are symmetrically placed at 25% and 75% of the alignment template. Unlike previous approaches like [7], which use input images of 60×60 pixels, our aligned image are resized to only 50×50 pixels.

Support Vector Regression. Given a training set with L data examples $\mathbf{X} \in \mathbb{R}^m$ and their outputs $\mathbf{Y} \in \mathbb{R}^1$, the standard formulation of SVR under a given regularization cost C and slack variables ϵ is defined as

$$\min_{\mathbf{w},b,\xi,\xi^*} \frac{1}{2}\mathbf{w}^T\mathbf{w} + C\left(\sum_{i=1}^{L}\xi_i + \sum_{i=1}^{L}\xi_i^*\right) \tag{1}$$

$$s.t. \ \mathbf{w}^T\phi(\mathbf{x}_i) + b - y_i \leq \epsilon + \xi_i$$
$$y_i - \mathbf{w}^T\phi(\mathbf{x}_i) - b \leq \epsilon + \xi_i^*$$

with $\xi_i, \xi_i^* \geq 0, i = 1 \ldots L$, where the kernel function $\phi(\mathbf{x_i})$ maps the feature vector $\mathbf{x_i}$ into a higher-dimensional space. This optimization problem is usually solved through its dual formulation, using algorithms such as Sequential Minimal Optimization.

Multilayer Neural Networks. The proposed MNN consists of an input visual feature layer, K hidden layers, and a single output neuron as an age regressor. All activation functions are set to be log-sigmoid, $\sigma(\beta, x) = \frac{1}{1+exp(-\beta x)}$. The prediction at layer k is

$$\mathbf{y}^{(k)} = \sigma(\mathbf{b}^{(k)} + \mathbf{\Theta}^{(k)}\mathbf{y}^{(k-1)}), \tag{2}$$

with $\mathbf{y}^{(1)} = \mathbf{b}^{(1)} + \mathbf{\Theta}^{(1)}\mathbf{x}$, where $\mathbf{x} \in \mathbf{X}$ is the input vector to the MNN, $\mathbf{b}^{(k)}$ a vector of unitary bias neurons and $\mathbf{\Theta}^{(k)}$ a matrix of connection weights. The cost function is

$$C(\mathbf{\Theta}) = \frac{1}{M}\left(-\mathbf{y}\log\mathbf{y}^{(K)} - (1 - \mathbf{y}^{(K)})\log(1 - \mathbf{y}^{(K)})\right) + \frac{\lambda}{2M}\sum_{k=1}^{K}\mathbf{\Theta}^{(k)2}, \tag{3}$$

where $\mathbf{y} \in \mathbf{Y}$ is the ground truth and λ prevents overfitting by ℓ_2-regularization. Due to the log-sigmoid activations, the output regressor is factorized by 100 to directly provide age estimates in the range $[0-100]$. Each backpropagation step is accomplished by iterative unconstrained minimization of the multivariate cost function $C(\mathbf{\Theta})$, using

$$\frac{\partial \sigma}{\partial \theta_i} = \beta \sigma(\beta, \theta_i)\left(1 - \sigma(\beta, \theta_i)\right) + \frac{\lambda}{M}\theta_i \tag{4}$$

as the multivariate gradient function for non-bias neurons. In our experiments, we used $\beta = 1$ and set the number of minimization iterations to 10.

Random Forests. Random forests are ensemble learners used for either classification or regression. The models are trained by applying bootstrap aggregation to N_{tree} base classification and regression trees. During the learning stage, each tree $h_n, n = 1, \ldots, N_{tree}$ samples with replacement a random selection of m-dimensional examples $(\mathbf{X}_B, \mathbf{Y}_B) \in (\mathbf{X}, \mathbf{Y})$. For each new grown node, a number $m_{try} \ll m$ of predictor variables θ are randomly selected, and the variable that provides the best binary split over the bootstrapped subset according to some objective function is selected for that node. A tree is grown until leaf nodes are pure, i.e. they consist of samples containing a single label. When presented with new data, each tree individually predicts an output, and a collective target response is provided by averaging or majority voting of the forest $\{h_n(\mathbf{X}, \theta_n)\}, \forall n$, for regression and classification problems, respectively.

Regularized Canonical Correlation Analysis. CCA is posed as the problem of relating data $\mathbf{X}$ to labels $\mathbf{Y}$ by finding basis vectors w_x and w_y such that the projections of the two variables on their respective basis vectors maximize the correlation coefficient

$$\rho = \frac{w_x{}^T \mathbf{X} \mathbf{Y}^T w_y}{\sqrt{(w_x{}^T \mathbf{X} \mathbf{X}^T w_x)(w_y{}^T \mathbf{Y} \mathbf{Y}^T w_y)}}, \tag{5}$$

or, equivalently, finding $\max_{w_x, w_y} w_x{}^T \mathbf{X} \mathbf{Y}^T w_y$ subject to the scaling $w_x{}^T \mathbf{X} \mathbf{X}^T w_x{=}1$ and $w_y{}^T \mathbf{Y} \mathbf{Y}^T w_y{=}1$. For age estimation, labels in $\mathbf{Y}$ are unidimensional, so a least squares fitting suffices to relate these labels to the projected data features. Thus, only w_x is computed, by solving the following generalized eigenvalue problem:

$$\mathbf{X} \mathbf{Y}^T \left((1 - \gamma_y)\mathbf{Y} \mathbf{Y}^T + \gamma_y I\right)^{-1} \mathbf{Y} \mathbf{X}^T w_x = \lambda \left((1 - \gamma_x)\mathbf{X} \mathbf{X}^T + \gamma_x I\right) w_x \tag{6}$$

Regularization terms $\gamma_x, \gamma_y \in [0, 1]$ have been included in Eq. 6 to prevent overfitting. Although CCA admits extension to a kernelized version, in that case covariance matrices become computationally intractable with over 10K samples. In practice, regularized CCA works comparably to KCCA [7], it is much less

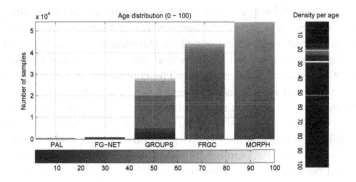

Fig. 2. Age distribution and density per database. In Age distribution the color represents the age. In Density per age the color represents the density (white color more density). PAL and FG-NET are relatively negligible compared to others, and GROUPS only provides age intervals, so we focus on MORPH II and FGRC. Age samples are mainly skewed towards people who are 20–30 and 50 years old.

computationally demanding, and will allow us to employ the same exact validation schemes over large databases.

4   Experimental Results

Age Databases. Due to the nature of the age estimation problem, there is a restricted number of publicly available databases providing a substantial number of face images labeled with accurate age information. The most well known examples in the literature are the PAL database [11], with 580 frontal images from non-repeated subjects; the FG-NET Aging Database [10], with 1,002 face images from 82 subjects; the GROUPS database, with 28,231 faces of non-repeated subjects; the Face Recognition Grand Challenge v2.0 (FRGC) database [15], with 44,278 images from 568 subjects; and the MORPH II database [16], with 55,134 face images of 13,618 subjects.

PAL and FG-NET are comparatively negligible to the rest in terms of number of samples. Additionally, age annotations in GROUPS are discretized into seven age intervals, which makes it unsuitable for training accurate age regression models. Moreover, FG-NET contains only 82 subjects, so a *leave-one-person-out* validation scheme is employed by convention, to avoid optimistic biasing by identity replication. Given such limitations, and the recent tendency to use MORPH as a standard for age estimation, we concentrate on this database and on FRGC to provide experimental evaluations. Although the FRGC database is comparable to MORPH regarding number of samples, image quality and age range coverage, we were not able to find any previous publication on age estimation including FRGC as part of their experiments. This new database for age estimation is described next. Figure 2 offers a graphical visualization and comparison of the analyzed databases, by number of samples and density of age ranges.

FRGC database [15] is presented in 2005 and contains approximately 50,000 images from 568 subjects. The database consists of four controlled still images, two uncontrolled still images, and one three-dimensional image for each subject session. Different sessions have been carried out during different years (2002, 2003, and 2004) with the same subjects. The controlled images were taken in a studio setting, are full frontal facial images taken under two lighting conditions (two or three studio lights). The uncontrolled images were taken in varying illumination conditions; e.g., hallways, atria, or outdoors. Each set of controlled and uncontrolled images contains two expressions, smiling and neutral. The 3D images were taken under controlled illumination conditions appropriate for the Vivid 900/910 sensor. For our experiments we have used the database without the 3D images, only 44k images. They are 56% male, and 44% female, 69% White, 1% Black, and 30% Asian. The age range is between $18 - 70$ years old, with a proportion 56% between $18 - 22$, 21% between $23 - 27$, and 23% more than 28+ years old.

Metrics. We adopt the conventional metrics of Mean Average Error (MAE) and Cumulative Score (CS) for comparison with recent literature. MAE computes the average age deviation error in absolute terms, $MAE = \sum_{i=1}^{M} |\hat{a}_i - a_i|/M$, with $\hat{a}_i$ the estimated age of the i-th sample (i.e. $y_i^{(K)}$ in the case of the MNN), a_i its real age and M the total number of samples. CS [1,8,19] is defined as the percentage of images for which the error e is no higher than a given number of years l, as $CS(l) = M_{e \leq l}/M$. Related publications typically supply either an eleven-point curve for age deviations $[0 - 10]$, or simply the value $CS(5)$. We provide both results for future reference.

The optimal HOG parameters were searched for so as to minimize the MAE score over MORPH, using 5-fold cross-validation. In particular, the division into training and validation sets was made so that all the instances of the same subject were contained in one single fold at a time; this applies to all the experiments presented in this paper. We found that the version of 8×8 and 9 bins per histogram granted the best results. In our experiments, HOG descriptors are extracted directly from the aligned version of each detected face. We observed that the best results were achieved by directly inputting the per-cell, unitary-normalized HOG descriptors, without any further normalization. The selected HOG feature has the advantage of being considerably more compact than other features commonly used in the literature. For instance, the BIF feature in [13] is 4376-dimensional, whereas ours is only 576. This results in faster convergence of the algorithm, less data complexity (deriving into fewer layers required), and a smoother regularization parameter space for a similar expressive power.

SVR experiments were carried out using the ϵ-SVR implementation from the LIBSVM library[1], with a Radial Basis Function kernel. All of our experiments employ the same input features, i.e. the signed version of unit-normalized HOG over an 8×8 grid and 9 encoding bins. The optimal regularization cost C, and hyper-parameters γ and ϵ have been independently obtained for each target database, through exhaustive logarithmic grid search and 5-fold cross-validation.

---

[1] http://www.csie.ntu.edu.tw/~cjlin/libsvm/

Table 1. Age estimation results in MORPH II for the compared algorithms and visual descriptors, in a variety of settings. Symbol (−) indicates unreported values

	MORPH-5CV			
Technique	Feature	Train/test	MAE	CS(5)
WAS [4,10]	AAM+BIF	55K	9.21	−
AAS [4]	AAS+BIF	55K	10.10	−
AGES [4,5]	AAM+BIF	55K	6.61	−
RED (SVM) [1]	AAM	6K	6.49	48.9%
OHRank [1]	AAM	6K	6.07	56.4%
OHRank [1,4]	AAM+BIF	55K	6.28	−
PLS [6,7]	BIF	10K/55K	4.56	−
kPLS [6,7]	BIF	10K/55K	4.04	−
IIS-LLD [4]	AAM+BIF	55K	5.67	−
CPNN [4]	AAM+BIF	55K	4.87	−
CCA [7]	BIF	10K/55K	5.37	−
rCCA [7]	BIF	10K/55K	4.42	−
kCCA [7]	BIF	10K/55K	3.98	−
MFOR [19]	PCA+LBP+BIF	4K	4.20	72.0%
SVM+SVR [8]	BIF+ASM	78K	4.20	72.4%
SVR	**HOG**	55K	4.83	63.4%
MNN	**HOG**	55K	7.91	34.0%
RF	**HOG**	55K	6.84	43.1%
rCCA	**HOG**	55K	4.84	64.1%

A similar grid search has been carried out for RF, in order to adjust the optimal parameters N_{tree} and m_{try}. In this case, the technique was particularly invariant to the choice of parameters.

The optimal architecture and regularization for the MNN have been explored through grid-search again, dividing the target database into 20 folds. Each MORPH subset contained over 3K samples, granting faster convergence.

Regarding CCA, only the regularization terms need to be optimized. Interestingly, the best choice of regularization turned out to be $\gamma_x = \gamma_y = 0$. This is explained by the size of the descriptor, which is orders of magnitude smaller than the number of examples ($576 \ll L$), and thus less prone to overfit the data.

Table 1 shows a thorough comparison with publications that supply cross-validation MAE using MORPH (referred as MORPH-5CV). Unlike many previous works [1,6,7,19], our MORPH-5CV experiment exploits the whole available set of 55K samples, by training from 4 folds, testing over the remaining one and averaging all five combinations.

Table 2 includes scores for FRGC as a future reference for the research community (FRGC-5CV). Furthermore, we feel that cross-database (CDB) generalization would be a challenging and interesting metric to take into account for validating the robustness of a method. For this reason, we additionally include the generalization scores obtained when training a whole database using its optimal 5CV parameters, and testing it completely with the other database. These

Table 2. MAE scores and CS(5) percentages from all four classification schemes for MORPH and FRGC, under the two validation scenarios

Validation scheme	MAE				CS(5)			
	SVR	ANN	RF	CCA	SVR	ANN	RF	CCA
MORPH–5CV	**4.83**	7.91	6.84	**4.84**	**63.4%**	34.0%	43.1%	**64.1%**
FRGC–5CV	**2.88**	4.34	4.08	4.41	**89.2%**	71.0%	82.1%	73.7%
MORPH→FRGC	7.55	7.47	8.92	**7.43**	41.3%	43.1%	30.5%	**44.8%**
FRGC→MORPH	**8.89**	8.90	9.51	8.50	**39.1%**	36.0%	33.6%	**39.1%**

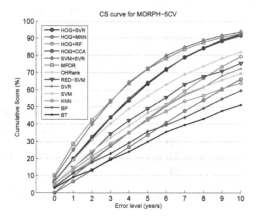

Fig. 3. Comparative of Cumulative Score curves from recent age estimation algorithms and our four evaluations: HOG+SVR, HOG+MNN, HOG+RF, HOG+CCA

appear in the aforementioned table as MORPH→FRGC and FGRC→MORPH, where the testing database appears last. These results also prove the good generalization properties of the evaluated techniques.

Figure 3 shows CS curves for the MORPH database, comparing our four evaluations with different published algorithms: BT, BP, kNN, SVM, SVR and RED-SVM [1]; OHRank[1]; MFOR [19]; and SVM+SVR [8]. In case of algorithm variations, best curves were chosen. Likewise, Figure 4 shows the CS curves of our proposed algorithms for MORPH and FRGC, both for 5CV and for the more challenging CDB validation scenario. Table 2 details CS(5) scores for these validation scenarios. For those works that facilitated the CS(5) score for the MORPH database, this metric has also been included for comparison in Table 1.

When comparing the accuracy of the techniques, we see that CCA and SVR perform similarly well, and comparable to state-of-the-art algorithms employing much more complex features and preprocessing. We have observed that MNN is very sensitive to particular weight initializations, RF is quite invariant to its parameterization. Regarding computational efficiency during training, the time lapse for a cross-validation fold is approximately 9 hours for SVR, 5 hours for

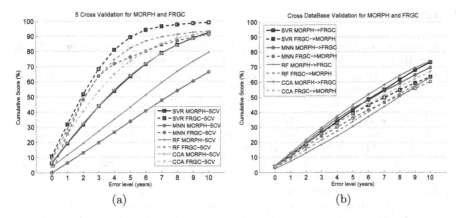

Fig. 4. Cumulative Score curves of the four evaluated techniques, for MORPH and FRGC, in (a) 5-fold cross-validation (5CV) and (b) cross-database validation (CDB) scenarios

RF, 9 min for MNN and 3 sec for CCA, on an Intel i7 computer at 1.6 GHz. This gives significant advantage to CCA.

5   Conclusions

We evaluated four machine learning techniques applicable to age regression from facial images: SVR, MNN, RF and CCA. We demonstrated that replacing complex feature extraction schemes with HOG features achieves comparable performance to the state-of-the-art, while being faster and easily replicable. Our approach requires less feature tuning; it does not involve statistical face models requiring precise annotation of tens of facial landmarks; and it does not require additional cues. During the method comparison, CCA and SVR similarly provided the best accurate results, although the combination of HOG+CCA proved to be the most computationally efficient and straight-forward, not even requiring parameter adjustment. Furthermore, we introduced FRGC as a suitable (and so far unnoticed) large database for age estimation, and proposed a cross-database validation scheme to test the generalization of age estimation methods. Further research should explore the incorporation of additional cues such as gender and ethnicity. These cues have been effectively used in the past to increase age estimation accuracy [7].

Acknowledgments. The authors would like to thank to Christina Zitello for English editing. This work has been partially supported by the Spanish Ministry of Science and Innovation (MICINN) through the Torres-Quevedo funding program (PTQ-11-04401).

References

1. Chang, K.-Y., Chen, C.-S., Hung, Y.-P.: Ordinal hyperplanes ranker with cost sensitivities for age estimation. In: CVPR, pp. 585–592. IEEE (2011)
2. Dalal, N., Triggs, B.: Histograms of oriented gradients for human detection. In: CVPR, vol. 1, pp. 886–893. IEEE (2005)
3. Fu, Y., Guo, G., Huang, T.S.: Age synthesis and estimation via faces: A survey. TPAMI 32(11), 1955–1976 (2010)
4. Geng, X., Yin, C., Zhou, Z.-H.: Facial age estimation by learning from label distributions. TPAMI 35, 2401–2412 (2013)
5. Geng, X., Zhou, Z.-H., Smith-Miles, K.: Automatic age estimation based on facial aging patterns. TPAMI 29(12), 2234–2240 (2007)
6. Guo, G., Mu, G.: Simultaneous dimensionality reduction and human age estimation via kernel partial least squares regression. In: CVPR, pp. 657–664. IEEE (2011)
7. Guo, G., Mu, G.: Joint estimation of age, gender and ethnicity: CCA vs. PLS. In: 10th Int. Conf. on Automatic Face and Gesture Recognition. IEEE (2013)
8. Han, H., Otto, C., Jain, A.K.: Age estimation from face images: Human vs. machine performance. In: International Conference on Biometrics (ICB). IEEE (2013)
9. Lanitis, A., Draganova, C., Christodoulou, C.: Comparing different classifiers for automatic age estimation. TSMC-B 34(1), 621–628 (2004)
10. Lanitis, A., Taylor, C.J., Cootes, T.F.: Toward automatic simulation of aging effects on face images. TPAMI 24(4), 442–455 (2002)
11. Minear, M., Park, D.C.: A lifespan database of adult facial stimuli. Behavior Research Methods, Instruments, & Computers 36(4), 630–633 (2004)
12. Montillo, A., Ling, H.: Age regression from faces using random forests. In: ICIP, pp. 2465–2468. IEEE (2009)
13. Mu, G., Guo, G., Fu, Y., Huang, T.S.: Human age estimation using bio-inspired features. In: CVPR, pp. 112–119. IEEE (2009)
14. Oro, D., Fernández, C., Saeta, R.J., Martorell, X., Hernando, J.: Real-time GPU-based face detection in HD video sequences. In: ICCV Workshops, pp. 530–537 (2011)
15. Jonathon Phillips, P., Flynn, P.J., Scruggs, T., Bowyer, K.W., Chang,, J., Hoffman, K., Marques, J., Min, J., Worek, W.: Overview of the Face Recognition Grand Challenge. In: CVPR, pp. 947–954. IEEE (2005)
16. Ricanek, K., Tesafaye, T.: MORPH: a longitudinal image database of normal adult age-progression. In: Automatic Face and Gesture Recognition, pp. 341–345 (2006)
17. Riesenhuber, M., Poggio, T.: Hierarchical models of object recognition in cortex. Nature neuroscience 2(11), 1019–1025 (1999)
18. Sun, Y., Wang, X., Tang, X.: Deep convolutional network cascade for facial point detection. In: CVPR, pp. 3476–3483. IEEE (2013)
19. Weng, R., Jiwen, L., Yang, G., Tan, Y.-P.: Multi-feature ordinal ranking for facial age estimation. In: AFGR. IEEE (2013)

Author Index

Printed in the United States
By Bookmasters